EVERYDAY CELEBRATIONS

From Scratch

MARIA PROVENZANO

HARPER HORIZON

Everyday Celebrations From Scratch

© 2022 Maria Provenzano

All rights reserved. No portion of this book may be reproduced, stored in a retrieval system, or transmitted in any form or by any means—electronic, mechanical, photocopy, recording, scanning, or other—except for brief quotations in critical reviews or articles, without the prior written permission of the publisher.

Published by Harper Horizon, an imprint of HarperCollins Focus LLC.

Any internet addresses, phone numbers, or company or product information printed in this book are offered as a resource and are not intended in any way to be or to imply an endorsement by Harper Horizon, nor does Harper Horizon vouch for the existence, content, or services of these sites, phone numbers, companies, or products beyond the life of this book.

Photography by Leslie Grow and Bree McCool.

ISBN 978-0-7852-4579-7 (Ebook)
ISBN 978-0-7852-4578-0 (HC)

Library of Congress Control Number: 2021950349

Printed in South Korea

22 23 24 25 26 SAM 10 9 8 7 6 5 4 3 2 1

To my parents and my grandpa Provenzano. Thank you for teaching me to connect through food, for always inspiring me to be creative, and for instilling in me the importance of family.

And to my husband and boys, who give me something to celebrate every day.

CONTENTS

INTRODUCTION

Blowing out birthday candles is one of the most dazzling activities in the world. There is something so pure and uplifting about making a toast, singing a song, having a bite of that special, tasty food. (I'm a believer that even a small taste of frosting has secret powers.) Epic milestones like birthdays and graduations, and big celebrations like Thanksgiving, will always command our attention. But what about the little moments: the smell of fresh-baked cookies, a handwritten note, an A on a test, sacred time with friends and family? When we think of celebrations, these may not be the first things that come to mind. We can overlook these moments because of important conference calls, afternoon PTA meetings, and, well, life! But when we slow down and remain present, those moments can become some of our most cherished memories.

Now what if we decided to make the most of these opportunities, both big and small, and celebrate them?

Seriously, let's celebrate!

My mission is to inspire you to seek creative ways to commemorate all the good in your life. We live in a world where so much is premade, where almost anything can be bought and delivered in twenty-four hours, and we often forget that using our time and imaginations to make something handmade is more special than anything we can buy. Rejoicing in everyday moments can teach us gratitude and help us take pride in a life well lived—a major lesson my mom taught me. She was all about making the little things important. When I was in fifth grade, I woke up feeling anxious the morning of a big test. I walked into the kitchen and saw that my mom had prepared a delicious breakfast spread for me along with a good luck charm and an encouraging note that read, "I know you can do it!" I enjoyed the homemade pancakes as well as the comforting feeling that the work I did was seen and appreciated and someone was rooting for me.

That's what celebrations are about: connecting with your family, friends, and loved ones.

Valuing and cherishing the small moments are beliefs passed down on my dad's side, too, with food as the star. The Provenzanos love food—and I mean *love* food. In 1919, my great-grandfather founded an Italian grocery store with his family in my hometown of Saginaw, Michigan. Grandpa Frank and his two brothers later ran the store. Provenzano's was known as a place of quality and integrity, and the stories about the shop seem magical. The air was filled with the aroma of fresh-made doughnuts on Sunday mornings, and the sound of friendly banter could be heard across the meat counter throughout the week. It was the only place you could find the most sought-after off-the-shelf spaghetti sauces in town. To this day, there is nothing like J&R Spaghetti Sauce, named after my great-grandparents, Jack and Rose. I remember being a kid and eating fresh doughnuts in the back with my sister while spinning on the stools. I saw firsthand that food creates memories, hard work matters, and relationships and connection to the community are important.

All of these experiences made me the celebration enthusiast I am today.

In *Everyday Celebrations From Scratch*, I share my family's love of everyday celebrations with you, including fun themes and elements you can incorporate into your next soiree and lighthearted encouragement to discover easy and innovative ways to enjoy life a little more. The foundations of celebrating, with pantry and craft essentials that can be used time and time again for tons of do-it-yourself (DIY) projects and tasty dishes, will allow you to confidently put together your very own everyday celebrations. The book's five sections—weeknight meals, family, friendship, sports, and seasons—define areas in our lives that are perfect for a touch of jollification. The recipes are simple and delicious (many standouts hailing from my Italian and Midwest roots), and the DIY projects are fun and achievable.

So here's to nailing that presentation, wine night with your friends, your kid's first soccer game of the season, and every day of the week that ends in *y*. This book is my official invitation to get the party started and celebrate those moments that weave together into the tapestry of a beautiful life.

MARIA'S FAVORITES FOR CELEBRATING EVERY DAY

As a dedicated do-it-yourselfer, I've found that the key to success, which I learned from my mom, is planning, organizing, and having the right tools. With that being said, you can make any area in your home function as a crafting space. Simply dedicate a place for your "creative" supplies, stock your shelves in the kitchen with the essential tools and ingredients, and you'll be in business. Keep these essentials on hand so that the second you are inspired, you will be encouraged to make the most of your creativity.

Author's Note

In my role as a lifestyle expert, I'm often sent products to review. Occasionally, I find outstanding products that I end up using all the time, and I am so pleased with these brands that I accept payment to help make them more visible to others. I recommend two of these products—Tulip fabric paints and La Gioiosa wines—for projects and celebrations throughout this book, and I hope that you come to love them as much as I do. I'm grateful for their support!

From Scratch

WITH MARIA PROVENZANO

CRAFT SUPPLIES

My most frequently asked question when it comes to crafting is "How do I get started?" My favorite thing to tell people is to pick one, just one, project and get the supplies for it. Once you are done with that project, pick one item from your materials to be an asset to the next project and build on that. Each time you complete a project, you will have something new that will inspire another one, and you will end up with an entire house full of supplies (kidding—sort of).

MATERIALS

- **Clay:** Clay is one of my favorite craft supplies because of its versatility. I like using oven-bake clay rather than air-dry, mostly because I am a very impatient crafter and don't like to wait too long for crafts to dry.
- **Felt:** Felt is, in my humble opinion, by far the easiest and most versatile fabric to use when crafting. It doesn't fray, it holds an adhesive well, it can be sewn, it comes in a variety of colors—shall I go on? I find myself grabbing sheets in colors I like every time I'm at the craft supply store because they are so inexpensive.
- **Foam core:** As a DIYer, I love having supplies that are a blank canvas that can be used in many ways, and foam core is just that. Also known as foam board, it's basically a piece of foam sandwiched together with two large poster boards. It's easy to cut with a craft knife and can be used in unlimited ways. Be sure when painting or using a spray adhesive on one side that you paint or spray the other side as well to avoid bowing.
- **Resin:** Okay, this isn't a must-have, but it's one of my favorites. If you do one resin project, you will see how much fun it is. Resin is used for so many things, from creating trays to making jewelry. The process of combining two liquid components to create something that hardens always feels like a science experiment.
- **Ribbons and twine:** These two items are good to have around for a variety of projects. From gift wrapping to setting tables, I always find myself reaching for a little ribbon or twine to add a last-minute festive touch.

ADHESIVES

- **Fabric glue:** Fabric glue is used specifically for fabric because it dries in a way that moves with the fabric instead of making the fabric stiff. It also allows fabric to be washed without losing the adhesive.
- **Glue gun:** Glue guns come in a range of options and prices. Cordless glue guns are my favorite. I like having one with a larger tip and the ability to use thick glue sticks for my bigger projects, as well as one with a small tip that uses smaller glue sticks for more intricate projects.
- **Mod Podge:** Mod Podge is the best thing ever! It serves so many purposes when crafting, such as sealing paint and glitter or serving as an adhesive on a variety of bases.

PAINT

- **Acrylic craft paint:** Paint is an essential craft supply that is used in more ways than I can count. I like to keep basic colors on hand, plus colors that I love. They always come in handy because just a simple coat of paint can change an entire project.

- **Fabric paint:** Not all paints are created equal. Make sure that whatever paint you use in your crafting is curated specifically for the medium you are using it on. Fabric paint should be used on fabric because it will not only be easier to work with but also lead to a better final product and allow the painted item to be washed and used in the way fabric is meant to be used. Tulip Brush-On Fabric Paints are formulated exclusively for fabrics, which dry soft and remain ultra-flexible, so your results won't crack or crumble with movement.[*]

- **Puff paint:** I am a product of '80s crafting, and you know what we used in the '80s for everything? Puff paint! It has stood the test of time and is still one of my favorite craft supplies to use today. You name it, I put puff paint on it. Whether you're creating T-shirts or mugs, Tulip Dimensional Fabric Paints dry flexible and are permanent but machine washable. Since I use puff paint with my kids a lot, I like to make sure I'm using a nontoxic paint, and Tulip Dimensional Fabric Paints not only check off that box but can be used by crafters of all ages and skill levels on everything: school crafts, apparel, canvas art, accessories, home decor, and so much more. They add fun dimensional texture that stands out on every project![*]

- **Spray paint:** Spray paint is one of the most fun craft supplies, and it makes such a big impact. I use spray paint whenever I can because it provides an even finish, dries much faster, and is much easier to work with than paint and a paintbrush.

TOOLS

- **Craft-cutting mat:** I recommend getting a cutting board designed specifically for crafting. I like having one with grids and measurements on it.

- **Craft knife (aka X-ACTO):** I use a craft knife for projects that include paper, foam core, and even clay, to name a few. The key to these knives are the blades because they are easily removed and replaced. For best results, always use a fresh blade.

- **Medium-size craft knife:** It is also good to have a regular, medium-size knife for crafting. I use it for cutting things like wax, crayons, or any other medium that doesn't require the precise cutting of the X-ACTO knife. It is the same as a kitchen knife but dedicated to crafting use only.

- **Cutting board:** I have many cutting boards in my kitchen, but it's always good to designate one to crafting as well. While I save my cutting mat for precise cutting with my craft knife, this cutting board is for things like cutting wax, rolling out clay, or any other cutting that is a little too rough or dirty for the cutting mat.

---

[*]   Sponsored product; see author's note on page ix.

- **Cutting machine:** Cutting machines have taken over the craft world. They completely elevate projects unlike anything else. You can create designs on your computer and attach them to a variety of materials, such as wood, clothes, or plastic.

- **Paintbrushes:** Truth be told, I go through paintbrushes like crazy. I have nice ones that I use for important projects, but most of the time, I use inexpensive ones. No matter which budget you choose, having a variety of sizes in your craft space is helpful.

- **Quality scissors—for fabric and other purposes:** Do you really need two different scissors for crafting and fabric? Yes, my friends, you do! Dedicating a pair of scissors specifically for fabric is necessary for clean lines and ease. Grab another pair of scissors, aka craft scissors, for basically everything else.

- **Rolling pin:** I mostly use rolling pins when I am working with clay, but I find myself using them more than I expect when I am crafting. Dedicate one rolling pin to your craft supplies so you do not have to worry about craft materials ending up in your baking.

- **Ruler:** I am oddly picky about my rulers. I like having a variety when possible. A large fabric ruler is great for, you guessed it, fabric. I often use smaller, clear rulers for smaller projects. A large metal ruler will also come in handy more than you think.

- **Tool kit:** A basic tool kit is good to have around for even the simplest crafting. You would be surprised at how often hammers, screwdrivers, nails, levels, and so on are needed. Take the guesswork out by getting a kit that is already put together. If there isn't a drill included, then I recommend getting a drill and some drill bits.

ORGANIZATION

- **Peg board:** A great way to organize your supplies.
- **Craft cart:** Perfect for small spaces or for kids.
- **Clear containers:** The easiest way to stay organized because you can see where everything goes.
- **Color coding:** Makes a space look extra organized, especially if everything is stored in clear containers.

KITCHEN TOOLS

Many of my favorite kitchen items are from my wedding registry. I feel like there should be a registry for simply entering the real world as an adult. Dear world, I do not need these things because I am married; I need them because I no longer live with my mom who has all the things!

- **Microplane:** I use my Microplane for zesting citrus, grating garlic, and grating cheese. This simple tool is a great way to elevate your dishes by adding tiny bits of flavor that pack a punch.

- **Mandoline:** Mandolines are a must! I find that most people do not have these in their homes, but they make a huge difference when it comes to creating uniform slices of food. A mandoline also helps with prep because it can drastically shorten the time it takes to cut food.
- **Good knives:** All chefs will tell you that knives are an extension of their hands. Having good, sharp knives creates a better end product, and they are easier to work with.
- **Food processor:** No joke, my mom has had her food processor for over thirty years. She always says that if you take care of your things, they will stand the test of time. I use mine for making things like pesto, scones, dressings, and sauces, to name a few.
- **Pancake griddle:** There is nothing worse than bad pancakes, am I right? Trying to keep the temperature consistent, trying to figure out how many fit into a skillet, all the issues that go into making pancakes unsuccessful can be solved by getting a pancake griddle. Make sure to grab one that offers a consistent temperature. It will make your wonderfully sweet weekends extra sweet.
- **Stand mixer:** My stand mixer is my best friend and all-time favorite kitchen item. My parents bought me one as a college graduation present; that's how much I wanted it. A stand mixer will elevate your baking to professional status. I use it for mashing potatoes and mixing eggs into pâte à choux, and, of course, I use the attachment to make homemade pasta.
- **Hand mixer:** A hand mixer is second to the stand mixer but definitely has its place in the kitchen. I tend to use the hand mixer for smaller items like whipped cream or zabaglione.
- **Mixing bowls:** These are a necessity in the kitchen. I use mixing bowls when preparing both cooking and baking recipes. The French term *mise en place*, which means "everything in its place," is a phrase chefs use to describe the process of setting out your materials ahead of time in order to prepare your meals efficiently. All you need are some mixing bowls.
- **Spatula:** Rubber spatulas are good for both cooking and baking. I like having a variety of shapes and sizes as they all serve different purposes. Have at least five in your kitchen for efficiency.
- **Offset spatula:** I use this small yet mighty tool for decorating cakes, spreading meringue and jelly, and many other tasks. This simple tool is worth having in the kitchen drawer.
- **Cookie scoops:** When making cookies, creating uniform dough balls is key to them all cooking evenly. I use these scoops for muffins, pancakes, cupcakes, frosting, bonbons, and so much more. Grab at least three different sizes. I promise, you won't be sorry.
- **Measuring cups (for both liquid and dry ingredients):** Yes, you need different ones! When measuring liquid ingredients, it's important to use liquid measuring cups. These look like a pitcher, allow the measuring to be read on the side, and are easy to pour. For dry ingredients, classic measuring cups work best.
- **Baking sheets:** I use my baking sheets for both baking and cooking. Flat baking sheets allow baked goods like cookies to slide off easily if needed. For roasting, I like to use rimmed baking sheets. This allows me to toss the items around without worrying they will slide off. I use a variety of sizes and recommend having three different styles and sizes in the kitchen.

- **Parchment paper, aluminum foil, and silicone mats:** All three of these items are good to have on hand. I use parchment paper for lining baking sheets, aluminum foil for higher-temperature roasting, and silicone mats for baking and decorating.
- **Rolling pin:** Rolling pins are my favorite kitchen item to collect. I have rolling pins that I use in the kitchen and others that I like to display. The day-to-day ones are great for rolling out cookie dough, pie dough, and just about anything that requires flattening. When it comes to display, I love the look of vintage rolling pins and the history they hold. When I see them, I often wonder what recipes they helped bring to life.

FOR IMPROMPTU CELEBRATIONS

Because this book is dedicated to celebrating everyday moments, you better believe I keep my favorite celebration essentials on hand and well stocked for whatever occasion arises! I welcome *all* the celebrations. Whether it's a weeknight dinner that turns into a festive fete or kid-friendly neighborhood meetup that turns into a backyard BBQ, I'm here (and ready) for it.

- **A fridge full of bubbles:** My go-to prosecco is La Gioiosa, which in Italian means "joyful"—the perfect match for our everyday celebration mood. Here are my favorites:
    - Chilled La Gioiosa Prosecco Rosé: Pink wine is always fun, and it's even better when it's bubbly. Talk about an instant celebration.[*]
    - Chilled La Gioiosa Prosecco: Everyday celebrations require a bubbly wine that can pair with just about anything and is also certified organic. La Gioiosa Prosecco created their wine with the everyday in mind—bubbly isn't just for celebrating life's big events; it's ideal for small celebrations and the little joys of each day![*]
- **Candles:** The perfect way to change the mood is to add in candlelight. It makes even a simple weeknight meal feel special.
- **Homemade Confetti (page 70):** I can't help but feel happier if confetti is involved.
- **White table linens:** These make any table feel dressy.
- **Pasta:** It's the perfect blank canvas that can be dressed up or dressed down for any occasion.
- **A freezer loaded with these items:**
    - Pesto (pages 51, 53, and 306)
    - Homemade Marinara Sauce (page 143)
    - Dough for Classic Chocolate Chip Cookies (page 215)

---

[*]   Sponsored product; see author's note on page ix.

Part One

Celebrating Weeknight Meals

Traditions form the foundation for our memories. The celebration of tradition is practiced in our religions, cultures, countries, and homes. Typically, rituals are reserved for holidays, as these are times when our society celebrates something that unites us. The beauty of tradition, though, is that you can create your own whenever you'd like! I think you can make the most meaningful traditions in the everyday moments and simple joys in life. Some of my most sacred childhood memories are centered around weeknight dinners at the table with my family. I look back on those meals and feel those moments were indeed the foundation for my relationships. I always felt supported and safe, and although those things may seem small, they have meant the most in my life.

I'm a big believer in taking note of the small things to keep spirits high and hopeful. Creating a special meal or craft one or two nights a week with family and friends can help build community. If we celebrate the little victories we've accomplished each day, we will not only take in the moment but also build confidence, motivation, and happiness one weeknight celebration at a time.

Choosing one day of the week when everyone in your circle (family, friends, roommates, or coworkers) gathers together with the same intention and purpose can become a beautiful tradition. Before you know it, you'll find yourself looking forward to these gatherings and dreaming up new ways to make each celebration even more memorable and festive. I encourage you to kick off your first gathering with one of the fun suggestions in the chapters ahead and get ready to start your own custom!

TAKEOUT THURSDAY

FRIDAY FETE

WONDERFULLY SWEET WEEKEND

MAKING
MESSES
MONDAY

As a mom of two kids, I know the importance of teaching my boys that it's okay to make messes; I even encourage them to do so! Let's face it: with little kids, messes are constant—sticky fingers and dirty faces come with the territory. But the reason I wanted to create Making Messes Monday was to show my kids that messes happen every day as we learn, play, and grow. I've found that when I let my boys dive right in and get excited, they become more interested in the kitchen and get a feel for the gooey, fun time that cooking can be. Messes aren't just for the kids, though. You won't believe how enjoyable it is to allow yourself to get a little dirty in the kitchen. My goal is to help you and your family create a few messes and memories of your own. Let's get messy!

Set the Scene

Set yourself up for a mess success! I highly encourage prepping for a messy meal. That way, you can breathe a sigh of relief and dive into the filthy fun without a worry. Prep for a mess by covering your table with butcher paper. This paper is food-grade, so you can trust it provides a safe surface. Plus, it makes for a creative doodling canvas for your crew. Once you're done, you can fold or crumple it up and throw it in the recycling bin. Making a mess has never been so enjoyable and easy to clean!

Get the kids involved in the prep. I love assigning my kids small tasks like measuring, using kids' knives to cut fruit, mixing, and setting the table—anything that makes them feel like they're part of the process. Giving them a task will add an extra element of ownership over the meal and togetherness when you sit down to enjoy your creation.

---

* Sponsored product; see author's note on page ix.

PAINTED AND PERSONALIZED PLACE MATS

The whole point of Making Messes Monday is to have creative freedom and for the kids to feel like they are a part of the night. Creating their very own place mats gives them ownership of their project, and they'll take pride in showcasing their artwork. These place mats are functional pieces of art that will brighten up the table. The best part? They are so fun to make that it doesn't matter if they get messy. Make sure to use nontoxic, fabric-friendly paints like Tulip Brush-On Fabric Paint and Tulip Dimensional Paint.* Once the place mat has seen enough messes, it's time to create a new piece of art. (photo page 7)

MAKES 1 PLACE MAT

Kraft or butcher paper
Fabric place mats, preferably in a lighter color
Disposable plate
Tulip Brush-On Fabric Paint*
Paintbrushes
Tulip Dimensional Paint*

Cover a work space with the kraft paper or butcher paper. Place the place mats onto the paper.

Pour the fabric paint onto a disposable plate or something similar. Use paintbrushes to create your art on the place mats.

Move the painted place mats to a safe place to dry.

Personalize the place mats by writing your names with Tulip Dimensional Paint or using a cutting machine to create the lettering.*

Tips

- I love decorating for the seasons, so why not add a creative touch to the table by making the place mats seasonal?
- It's important to use fabric paint when painting on fabric. This will provide the best result that lasts and doesn't crumble off. With a variety of Tulip Brush-On Paint colors and a neutral-colored place mat, you can create endless ideas for how to customize or personalize your place settings.
- Add water to the paint to achieve a watercolor look.

---

* Sponsored product; see author's note on page ix.

LOADED VEGGIE NACHOS

It's been a mission of mine to create a recipe that evenly distributes each ingredient onto every individual bite, because there's nothing more frustrating than getting an empty chip out of a pile of nachos. My solution? A lovely Cheese Sauce that you'll want to swim in after tasting! The best thing about these nachos, aside from the even distribution of ingredients, is that they're customizable. Add any veggies, meat, or toppings you like. (photo pages 10–11)

MAKES 4 TO 6 SERVINGS

2 cups peeled and cubed sweet potatoes (1/2-inch cubes)

4 to 5 tablespoons olive oil, divided

1 teaspoon salt, divided

1 teaspoon Easy Taco Seasoning (page 32)

1 red onion, diced

1 red bell pepper, chopped into 1/2-inch pieces

1 cup zucchini, cut into 1/2-inch pieces

1 (15-ounce) can black beans, drained and rinsed

1 (12-ounce) bag corn tortilla chips

Cheese Sauce (page 12)

Garnish options: Guacamole (page 12) or diced avocados, sliced cherry tomatoes, roughly chopped cilantro, lime slices, sour cream, salsa

Preheat the oven to 425 degrees. Place the sweet potatoes on a half-sheet baking pan lined with aluminum foil, and drizzle with 2 tablespoons of the olive oil, 1/2 teaspoon of salt, and the taco seasoning. Toss to evenly coat the potatoes with the oil and seasoning and space them out on the baking sheet so they aren't crowded. Roast for about 15 to 20 minutes or until cooked through.

Lower the oven temperature to 400 degrees.

Heat the remaining 2 to 3 tablespoons of olive oil in a large skillet. Add the onions, bell peppers, and remaining 1/2 teaspoon of salt and cook over medium-high heat until the vegetables start to soften. Add the zucchinis and continue to cook until the veggies soften and slightly char. Stir in the black beans and remove from heat.

Line a rimmed half-sheet baking pan with aluminum foil. Place the tortilla chips on the baking sheet in a single layer. Sprinkle evenly with the veggie mixture and the sweet potatoes. Drizzle with the Cheese Sauce. Bake for about 10 minutes or until everything is hot and bubbly.

Garnish nachos as desired with Guacamole or diced avocados, sliced cherry tomatoes, roughly chopped cilantro, lime slices, sour cream, and/or salsa. Serve warm and crispy!

Tips

- Give each guest an individual sheet pan so they can easily customize their nachos.
- Pack in the protein by adding chicken or ground beef to the mix.
- Add in seasonal veggies, like peas in the spring and butternut squash in the fall.
- The Cheese Sauce and veggies can be cooked ahead of time and stored in the fridge until you're ready. I recommend heating the sauce in a pot on the stove. If the sauce is too thick, you can slowly add a little stock or milk to loosen it up.
- This is a great recipe to have in your pocket when you need a gluten-free option that is also an instant crowd-pleaser.

CHEESE SAUCE

MAKES APPROXIMATELY 1 1/2 CUPS

2 tablespoons unsalted butter

2 tablespoons all-purpose flour

1/4 teaspoon ground cumin

1/4 teaspoon chili powder

1/4 teaspoon garlic powder

1/4 teaspoon cayenne pepper, optional

1 cup whole milk, slightly warm

1 (8-ounce) block Monterey Jack cheese, grated

Salt and white pepper to taste

Melt the butter in a medium pot over medium heat. Add the flour and cook for about a minute, stirring constantly.

In a small bowl, mix together the cumin, chili powder, garlic powder, and cayenne (if desired). Add the spices into the butter mixture and cook for about 20 to 30 seconds, stirring constantly.

Whisk in the milk slowly. Continuing to whisk, turn the heat to medium-high and allow the mixture to get bubbly and thick.

Stir in the cheese and mix until it is well combined. Stir in the salt and white pepper, and adjust any seasonings as desired. Serve while warm.

Tip

Need to stall a bit? No problem! Place a piece of plastic wrap over the top of the sauce to prevent skin from forming, then use a fork to whip it up before serving.

GUACAMOLE

MAKES ABOUT 2 1/2 CUPS

2 ripe avocados, lightly mashed

2 tablespoons finely chopped red onion

1 jalapeño pepper, seeds removed, finely chopped

1/2 to 1 teaspoon crushed red pepper flakes, optional

2 tablespoons fresh lime juice

1/2 cup chopped cherry tomatoes

1/2 cup chopped fresh cilantro, divided

Salt and pepper to taste

In a bowl combine the avocados, red onions, jalapeños, crushed red pepper (if desired), lime juice, and cherry tomatoes.

Mix with a fork, but do not overmix; it is good to still have texture and bigger pieces of avocado.

Fold in 1/3 cup of the fresh cilantro. Add salt and pepper to taste.

Top the finished guacamole with the remaining fresh cilantro.

ITALIAN-STYLE CHICKEN FINGERS

Raise your hand if chicken fingers played a significant role in your childhood. Me too! Around my house, they weren't known as "chicken fingers" or "chicken nuggets." My mom made them from scratch, so we called them "breaded chicken bites." Her Italian-style version made in our house included herbs and, of course, Parmesan cheese. Instead of covering them with marinara sauce or dipping them in ketchup, we dipped them in jelly. You heard me right: jelly! The homemade chicken recipe became a staple I continue to serve today. It doesn't matter what you call them—they're a crowd-pleaser! (photo page 15)

MAKES 4 TO 6 SERVINGS

1 cup flour

2 large eggs

2 tablespoons milk

1 cup bread crumbs

1/2 cup freshly grated Parmesan cheese

2 tablespoons fresh flat-leaf parsley, finely chopped

1 tablespoon sesame seeds, optional

4 boneless, skinless chicken breasts, pounded to an even thickness and cut into long strips

1 teaspoon salt

1/4 teaspoon pepper

1/2 to 1 cup oil (coconut, olive, or sunflower), depending on the pan size

Place the flour in a shallow, wide bowl. Crack the eggs into a different shallow bowl, add the milk, and whisk until well combined. Place the bread crumbs, cheese, parsley, and sesame seeds (if desired) in a third shallow bowl.

Dry the chicken with a paper towel. This helps the flour stick better and creates a crunchier final product. Sprinkle the chicken with salt and pepper.

Dip one piece of chicken into the flour and turn it until it is lightly coated; tap off the excess flour. Dip chicken into the egg mixture until it is evenly coated. Dip chicken into the bread crumb mixture and coat completely. Tap off excess bread crumbs. Place the breaded chicken on a cooling rack to prevent the bottom from getting soggy as you prepare the rest of the chicken. Repeat with the remaining pieces of chicken.

Preheat the oven to 350 degrees.

After all the chicken pieces are coated, heat the oil in a frying pan. Use any oil with a high smoke point. You want the oil to be about 1/4 inch deep in the pan. Make sure the oil is hot enough by dropping in a few bread crumbs; if they immediately sizzle, the oil is ready.

Place a few of the breaded chicken pieces in the oil, making sure not to crowd the pan. Cook the chicken for a few minutes, until golden brown, then flip the pieces and cook the other side until golden brown. Place the chicken on an oven-safe cooling rack that fits into a baking sheet. Repeat with the rest of the chicken pieces.

Bake the chicken on the cooling rack over the baking sheet for about 10 minutes (or up to 20 minutes for larger pieces of chicken). Remove the baking sheet from the oven and allow the chicken to sit for 5 to 10 minutes. Serve hot, preferably with melted jelly (I know it's weird, but it's good), honey, ketchup, Honey Mustard (page 14), or Herby Ranch (page 14).

Tips

- Season the chicken before dipping. This allows the flavors to absorb into the chicken.
- Using shallow dishes for dipping makes the process easier and helps better coat the chicken.
- For an extra crispy crust, let the coated chicken sit in the fridge on a cooling rack for a couple of hours before frying.
- Add a dash of salt right after cooking in the oil. It adds a nice texture and sticks well to the freshly fried chicken.
- Don't skip the step of baking in the oven. Baking finishes the cooking process and allows the juices to settle, which makes the outside crunchy and prevents the inside from getting dry.
- If you want to try dipping these Italian-Style Chicken Fingers in jelly like my family used to, my favorite flavors are raspberry, currant, or a blend of the two (page 147). I like to melt the jelly in the microwave so it is liquidy and warm when dipping.

HONEY MUSTARD

MAKES ³/4 CUP

1/3 cup Dijon mustard

1/4 cup honey

1/4 cup mayonnaise

1 tablespoon lemon juice

1/4 teaspoon cayenne pepper, optional

Whisk together the Dijon mustard, honey, mayonnaise, lemon juice, and cayenne (if desired). Adjust flavors to suite your palate.

HERBY RANCH

MAKES 2 1/2 CUPS

1 cup mayonnaise

1/2 cup sour cream

1 cup buttermilk

2 to 3 tablespoons lemon juice

1 teaspoon garlic powder, or 2 garlic cloves, minced

1 shallot, finely minced

2 tablespoons finely chopped fresh parsley

1 tablespoon finely chopped fresh dill

1 tablespoon finely chopped fresh chives

1/4 teaspoon salt

1/4 teaspoon pepper

Whisk together the mayonnaise, sour cream, buttermilk, and lemon juice.

Whisk in the garlic and shallot.

Gently whisk in the parsley, dill, chives, salt, and pepper.

Adjust seasonings to taste.

STICKY OVEN-BAKED BBQ RIBS

When it comes to making messes, ribs are at the top of the list! I like mine loaded with sauce—the messier, the better. To make tender ribs with caramelized edges, cooking them in the oven low and slow is your best bet. Ribs are actually a pretty easy "set it and forget it" meal; you can pop them in the oven while you're getting work done, helping with homework, or cleaning up the house so it doesn't look like a tornado hit it.

MAKES 4 TO 6 SERVINGS

4 pounds baby back pork ribs, membrane removed

2 teaspoons salt

1 teaspoon pepper

2 1/2 cups Jojo's BBQ Sauce (page 17), divided, or more as desired for serving

Pat the ribs dry with a paper towel and place them on a baking sheet lined with aluminum foil. Sprinkle the ribs with the salt and pepper, massaging the seasoning into the meat. Pour 2 cups of the BBQ sauce over the ribs, making sure to slather both sides.

Cover the ribs loosely with aluminum foil and bake for about 1 1/2 hours or until the meat is tender. Slather on the remaining 1/2 cup of BBQ sauce when the meat is cooked.

To create a nice crust on the outside of the ribs, grill them for about 5 minutes per side or broil them in the oven for 2 to 5 minutes. Serve hot with extra sauce.

Tips

- Removing the membrane on the ribs is controversial. I like to have it removed when I purchase the meat from the butcher to save time and effort.
- Make the ribs ahead by cooking them in the oven and letting them cool completely. Store them in the fridge in an airtight container. When you're ready to serve, you can grill your ribs to heat them up or place them under the broiler.
- My favorite side dishes to serve with ribs are mashed potatoes and corn on the cob.

JOJO'S BBQ SAUCE

MAKES ABOUT 7 CUPS

2 tablespoons olive oil

1 large onion, finely chopped

1/2 teaspoon salt

1 1/2 cups firmly packed
light brown sugar

2 tablespoons Worcestershire sauce

1 1/2 tablespoons yellow mustard

1 tablespoon chili powder

3/4 cup cider vinegar

32-ounce bottle ketchup

2 cups beef broth

Heat the oil in a medium saucepan and add the onions and salt. Cook until the onions soften, stirring frequently.

Stir in the brown sugar, Worcestershire sauce, mustard, chili powder, and cider vinegar until thoroughly combined. Cook for about a minute until fragrant.

Stir in the ketchup and beef broth. Bring to a boil, then reduce to a simmer for about 30 minutes.

Allow the mixture to cool slightly. Use an immersion blender (or pour it into a regular blender) to blend until smooth.

Cool completely before placing in a sealed container and storing in the fridge until ready to use. This will stay good in the fridge for 5 to 7 days.

Tips: Actually Make a Mess!

Here are ideas for making a mess without the stress:

- Be prepared! Make sure your table is covered and napkins are readily available.
- Plan ahead when you can. I like to get my kids involved in the planning process—whether that's grocery shopping or writing out the dinner plans for the week. It's good to teach them that meals take time and effort.
- Follow the motto: "We made a mess; now we clean it up." I am a huge advocate for allowing kids to be messy when they cook or craft. I also think there is a lesson in the act of cleaning it all up. This shouldn't feel like a punishment; it should just feel like part of the process of the night. Listening to music or chatting as a family can also connect us while we are cleaning up!

TACO TUESDAY

Taco Tuesday may be the most popular meal-planning theme night ever, and I'm here for it! It's the meal that gives us that little incentive to keep going, and for us adults it typically comes with a margarita. Win-win. At my house, Taco Tuesday is always a unanimous hit, which, for any mom of picky eaters, is cause for celebration in itself.

I love how taco recipes can be intricate or simple. Either way, I feel accomplished when I see how much joy the meal brings to my family. The benefits of sharing a meal with family always warms my heart, and even though dinners can fly by, those precious minutes are well worth the effort.

My goal in this section is to help you branch out a bit and explore new cuisines or add a unique element to your favorite dish. Fresh ingredients or a particular craft can add an unexpected twist to provide everyday celebration fun that you won't soon forget. Get ready to take Taco Tuesday to the next level.

Set the Scene

Adding bright colors to a weeknight dinner instantly imparts an element of cheer. For Taco Tuesdays, instead of a tablecloth, I lay out a Mexican serape, a blanket with bright colors and designs that's a nice change of pace from our everyday tablecloth.

Make your store-bought flower bouquet go a long way! One of the best items you can have in your supplies is a variety of bud vases. Spread them along your table or buffet and place a flower or two in them. This looks sweet and effortless. After dinner, you can station the vases around your home and enjoy them the rest of the week.

Also consider placing fresh citrus on your table as an easy way to add color and freshness. I love including citrus to almost any recipe, so this element can serve as both decor and additional flavoring for your food.

POM-POM NAPKIN RINGS

Pom-poms bring happiness! I mean, can you look at a pom-pom and be sad? No. I'm a sucker for this craft staple because it adds an element of playfulness to any project. Once you learn how to make these cute little puffs, the world of crafting will open up to you. I've used pom-poms on everything from garlands to wall decor. It's amazing how something so simple can make such a big impact. Here are three easy ways to incorporate this staple into your DIY repertoire. (photo page 18)

MAKE POM-POMS USING A FORK

This technique is good for small pom-poms.

MAKES 1 POM-POM

Yarn/wool

Small or large fork (depending on your desired pom-pom size)

Fabric scissors

Use your thumb to hold the yarn in place at the center of the fork. Wrap the yarn around the prongs about 50 times or until you've reached your desired thickness. Leave a slight gap at the bottom of the prongs. Cut the yarn.

Cut a new piece of yarn about 6 to 8 inches long. Thread it through the center tines, and tie a knot to hold it in place. Gently slide the yarn off the fork, tie the knot tighter, and double knot.

Cut the loops on either side to create the pom-pom. Trim the yarn so the ends are even and the pom-pom is puffy and rounded.

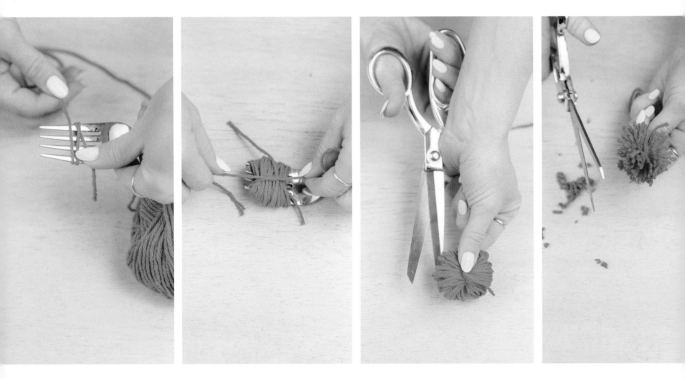

MAKE POM-POMS USING CARDBOARD

This method allows you to customize your pom-pom size. Make the cardboard template as wide as the finished pom-pom will be. To make a 4-inch pom-pom, the cardboard should be 4 inches wide top to bottom.

MAKES 1 POM-POM

1 small piece of cardboard, cut to the size of the desired pom-pom

Craft scissors

Yarn/wool

Fabric scissors

With craft scissors, cut your cardboard in a rectangle as wide as you want your pom-pom to be. Cut a 1- to 2-inch notch in the center.

Wrap the yarn around the middle of the cardboard until you reach the desired thickness. Cut the yarn with fabric scissors.

Cut a new piece of yarn about 12 inches long. Thread it through the notch perpendicular to the wrapped yarn, then tie the yarn in a secure knot. Slide the yarn off the cardboard and tie the knot tighter and double knot.

Cut the loops on both sides to create the pom-pom. Trim the yarn so the ends are even, puffy, and round.

MAKE POM-POMS USING A PAPER TOWEL ROLL

This technique is good for creating larger pom-poms.

MAKES 1 POM-POM

Craft scissors
1 paper towel roll
Yarn/wool
Fabric scissors

Using your craft scissors, cut a paper towel roll in half.

Holding the two halves together so they look like a pair of binoculars, wrap the yarn around the two tubes until you've reached the desired thickness. Cut the yarn with fabric scissors.

Cut another piece of yarn about 10 inches long and tie it in a loose knot around the center where the two rolls meet. Carefully slide the yarn off the tubes and tie a tight double knot.

Cut the loops on both sides to create the pom-pom. Trim the yarn ends with scissors to make them even and fluffy.

POM-POM NAPKIN RING

MAKES 1 RING

Hot-glue gun

Plain napkin ring

Yarn/wool

Fabric scissors

2 or 3 pom-poms; whichever size you
like that will fit on the napkin ring

Apply a small dot of hot glue on the center of the napkin ring, then begin to wrap the yarn around it to cover the circle. As you wrap, you can use the hot glue to secure the yarn (optional).

After the napkin ring is covered, cut the yarn from the yarn roll and secure the end of the yarn with hot glue.

Glue the pom-poms onto the ring with the hot glue.

Alternatively, tie a variety of pom-poms together and glue or tie them on the ring.

Tips

- Use thinner yarn for smaller pom-poms and thicker yarn for larger pom-poms.
- Brush the ends of the pom-poms with a bristle brush to make them look fluffier and rounder.
- To make your pom-poms equal in size, keep track of how many times you wrapped the yarn around the base.

SLOW-COOKER CHICKEN TACOS WITH OVEN-BAKED CRUNCHY SHELLS

When it comes to dinner prep, a slow cooker is your best friend. On days when I'm up at five in the morning, out the door with the kids by eight, and not home again until six in the evening, I feel relieved when I arrive home and have a hot, fresh dinner waiting for me—made from scratch. These Slow-Cooker Chicken Tacos are rich and tender from the flavors cooking together low and slow all day. Making the taco shells crunchy is entirely optional but totally worth it.

This recipe is another freezer favorite. Thaw them in the fridge the day you want to eat them, then heat them up when dinnertime rolls around.

MAKES 10 TO 12 8-INCH TACOS

Cooking spray

1 1/2 to 2 pounds chicken breast, sliced into very thin strips

1 red onion, sliced into thin strips

3 bell peppers, sliced into thin strips

1 (12-ounce) can black beans, drained and rinsed

2 tablespoons fresh lime juice plus additional lime wedges for topping

1/4 cup avocado oil or olive oil

2 cloves fresh garlic, minced

2 tablespoons Easy Taco Seasoning (page 32)

1 1/2 teaspoon salt

10 to 12 (8-inch) flour tortillas

8 to 10 tablespoons olive oil

12 tablespoons shredded Mexican-style cheese

TOPPINGS

Tangy and Crunchy Mayo-Free Slaw (page 28)

Sour cream

Fresh salsa

Guacamole (page 12)

Cotija cheese

Fresh cilantro, chopped

Lightly coat the bowl of the slow cooker with cooking spray or two tablespoons of olive oil. Add the chicken, onions, bell peppers, and black beans to the slow cooker.

In a separate bowl, whisk together the lime juice, avocado oil, garlic, taco seasoning, and salt. Pour the mixture over the chicken, onions, and peppers. Toss to coat well.

Cover and cook on high for 2 to 3 hours or on low for 4 to 6 hours, or until the chicken is cooked through.

Preheat the oven to 425 degrees. Place the tortillas on a half-sheet baking pan or baking sheet, lined with aluminum foil. Drizzle enough olive oil over the tortillas to evenly coat each side of the shells with olive oil. Place about 1 tablespoon of cheese along with about 1/3 cup of the chicken mixture onto half of the tortilla so that the other half can fold over; exact amounts will vary based on the size of the tortilla used. Repeat until all the tortillas are filled and folded.

Bake in the oven for about 10 minutes, then flip the tacos over and cook about 10 more minutes or until both sides are crispy.

Remove the tacos from the oven. Once they are cool enough to handle, add toppings and a fresh squeeze of lime onto the tacos and enjoy while they are hot.

Tips

- Use a variety of bell peppers. Each color offers a different flavor and adds dimension to the tacos.
- If you don't have a slow cooker, you can make this on your stove top as a skillet-style fajita. Sauté the bell peppers and onion over high heat to get a great char. Cook the chicken separately, then toss everything together with the taco seasoning.
- Try adding some cotija cheese, which is salty and similar to feta.
- To make these without the crunchy shells, use tongs to place the filling onto taco shells or soft tacos and add toppings.

TANGY AND CRUNCHY MAYO-FREE SLAW

MAKES ABOUT 3 CUPS

1 (9-ounce) bag red and green cabbage mixed with carrots

1 tablespoon cider vinegar

1/4 cup olive oil

2 teaspoons honey; more to taste

1/4 cup freshly chopped cilantro or parsley

Salt and pepper to taste

Place the cabbage mix, cider vinegar, olive oil, honey, and cilantro in a large bowl and toss together. Add salt and pepper to taste.

HOMEMADE WAFFLE CONE DESSERT TACOS

Nothing compares to the smell of fresh waffle cones being made at an ice cream shop. It's one of my favorite smells in the world, and you can create it in your home with some simple ingredients. My son Grant loves ice cream, and to make our Taco Tuesday extra special, I like to turn one of his favorite sweet treats into—you guessed it!—a taco. (photo page 30)

MAKES 7 TO 8 CONES

2 egg whites

Pinch of salt

7 tablespoons sugar

1 teaspoon vanilla extract

2/3 cup flour, divided

3 tablespoons unsalted butter, melted and cooled

Cooking spray or extra melted butter

Ice cream

In a stand mixer with a whisk attachment (or in a bowl using a hand mixer), whisk the egg whites, salt, and sugar on medium speed until the egg whites become lighter in texture. Stir in the vanilla extract.

With the mixer on low, mix in about half of the flour until just combined. Pour in the butter and mix until just combined. Add the rest of the flour and mix until just combined.

Heat the waffle cone press. Gently spray the press with cooking spray or lightly brush it with butter. Pour 1 to 2 tablespoon-size scoops of batter into the center of the waffle cone press (amount will vary based on the size of your waffle maker). Click the waffle press shut. After the timer goes off, remove the cooked batter and place it into a taco holder or on a homemade rack to create a taco shape.

Once the tacos are cooled, fill them with ice cream. For best results, soften the ice cream and scoop it into a piping bag, then pipe the ice cream into the waffle cones. Freeze the filled cones and take them out right after dinner. It's a helpful way to make dessert ahead of time.

I also like to serve these with a chocolate shell. You can add this right before serving by making a chocolate sauce that will harden once you dip the cold ice cream into it.

HARD SHELL CHOCOLATE SAUCE

MAKES ABOUT 1 CUP

10 ounces chocolate chips

2 tablespoons coconut oil

Make a double boiler by placing a heatproof bowl over a pan with simmering water, ensuring the water isn't touching the bowl.

Place the chocolate chips and coconut oil in the bowl, and let the ingredients slowly melt, stirring occasionally. Allow the chocolate to cool slightly before pouring it over the ice cream or dipping a waffle taco into it.

Tips

- A waffle cone press or pizzelle iron is necessary for a classic waffle shape. If you don't have either of these, you can make the taco shells in a skillet by placing it on medium heat, pouring 1 1/2 tablespoons of the batter into the warm skillet, and spreading the batter into a thin, even layer. Move it around fast to form a circle shape, roughly 6 x 6 inches. Cook for 4 to 5 minutes or until the base has set; flip, and continue to cook for 1 to 2 minutes. You want both sides to be nicely golden.
- If you don't have a taco holder, create the taco shell shape by hanging the cooked batter over a couple of wooden spoons placed between two objects, so the shell sides dangle down.
- If you want to shape the waffles into cones, lift the cooked batter off the waffle press or griddle and carefully and quickly roll it from the bottom around the cone mold or a similar funnel shape. Allow the cone to cool seam-side down to maintain its shape.
- Instead of rolling the cone or shaping it into a taco, you also can break the cooked batter into pieces to create "chips."

Tips: Forget-the-Frills Make-Ahead Tacos

Like the Boy Scouts say, "Always be prepared." I like to apply this philosophy to meals too. That's why I'm sharing this no-frills taco recipe that can be made days ahead and then warmed when ready. Gear up for a hectic work week by prepping these simple taco ingredients and stocking them in the fridge. Now all you have to do is minutes' worth of assembly, and voilà—you have a mouthwatering meal!

MAKES 4 SERVINGS

3 bell peppers, sliced, or 3 cups veggies of choice (my go-tos are bell peppers and zucchini)

1 onion, thinly sliced

1 teaspoon Easy Taco Seasoning

1 1/2 teaspoon salt, divided

1 cup beans of your choice, optional

1 pound ground beef or ground turkey

Taco shells or tortillas

In a large skillet, cook the onion and veggies with the taco seasoning and 1/2 teaspoon of salt until the veggies have softened and started to char.

Add the beans if you want a vegetarian option. I like to cook mine with the veggies so they absorb flavor from the taco seasoning. If you go this route, cook for an additional 5 minutes or until heated through.

Allow everything to cool, then store in an airtight container in the fridge.

Cook the ground beef in a large skillet with 1 tablespoon of olive oil and 1 teaspoon of salt. Cook until meat is at the desired doneness (or cooked through if it's turkey). I like to make sure the meat is nicely browned for added flavor. Allow the meat to cool completely and store it in an airtight container in the fridge.

When ready, heat up one serving of the ingredients and add to a taco shell or tortilla to make a single taco, or heat up the entire batch for an effortless dinner made from scratch!

EASY TACO SEASONING

MAKES ABOUT 3 TABLESPOONS

1 tablespoon chili powder

1/4 teaspoon garlic powder

1/2 teaspoon crushed red pepper flakes, more or less to taste

1/2 teaspoon dried oregano

1/2 teaspoon paprika

1 1/2 teaspoons ground cumin

1 teaspoon sea salt

1 teaspoon black pepper

Combine the chili powder, garlic powder, crushed red pepper, oregano, paprika, cumin, salt, and black pepper in a container with a fitted lid.

Stir together or place the lid on the container and shake well to combine.

PASTA WEDNESDAY

It's no coincidence that a man who loves pasta as much as my grandpa Frank became one of the most significant sources of inspiration in my life. Even when Grandpa Frank was working every day running Provenzano's grocery store with his brothers, he found a way to bring everyone together each week, under one roof and at one table, through one special menu item. You guessed it: pasta! Every Wednesday, Grandpa Frank worked only a half day at Provenzano's, and the family would all sit down together and have pasta. Until my dad went to college, he thought that all families celebrated Wednesdays with pasta.

I love feeling connected to these stories from my past through food. Pasta might be a simple ingredient, but it holds a sacred place in my heart. I feel like I'm sharing an old tradition and creating new memories with my family each week when we gather around one of my pasta creations.

Set the Scene

Many Italians love to decorate with food. I use the empty cans from making pasta sauce and fill them with fresh herbs. Using herbs instead of flowers adds to the meal experience because the scents harmonize instead of compete. I love to load the table up with additional food items, such as cherry tomatoes, breadsticks, and fresh lemons. I also think there's something special about lighting candles during dinnertime. I like to place unscented candles into mason jars and arrange them around the center of the table to create a deconstructed centerpiece along with the food and herbs. If you have young kids around, battery-powered lights are a safe alternative.

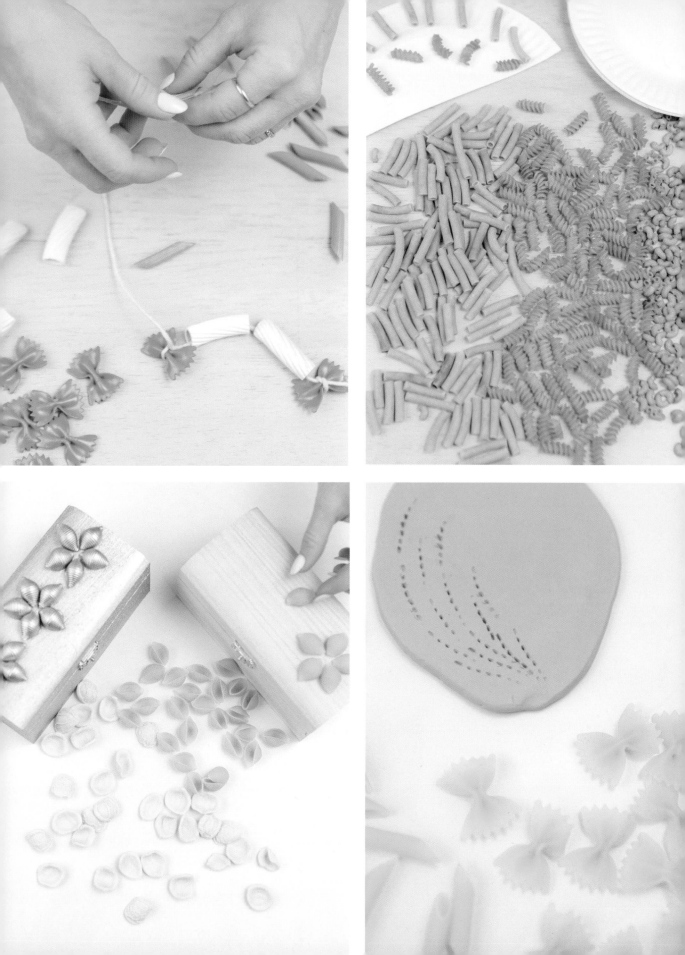

USE YOUR NOODLE: FOUR FUN WAYS TO PLAY WITH YOUR PASTA

I'm always looking for ways to entertain my family while I make dinner. Whether I make the meal in advance or I have as little as fifteen minutes to prep, they sit there and stare at me until the food is ready. Since we're celebrating pasta, why not use it to keep them busy and encourage them to be creative?

PAINTING PASTA NECKLACES

MAKES 1 NECKLACE

Nontoxic paint

A few handfuls of dried pasta with holes in the center

Paintbrushes

String

Baking sheet lined with wax paper

Working on a covered surface, paint the pasta with a paintbrush.

Place the painted pasta on a baking sheet lined with wax paper and set aside to dry completely.

After the pasta is completely dry, string it to make a necklace. Double knot the string.

Tips

- Cover your work surface with butcher paper or wax paper.
- Make sure the necklace string is long enough to fit over the head of the person who will wear it.
- If your kids are young, use washable nontoxic paint.

PAPER PLATE PASTA ART AND HOW TO DYE PASTA

MAKES 3 TO 5 CUPS DYED PASTA

3 to 5 cups of a variety of dried pasta

Container with a tight-fitting lid

Food coloring

1 teaspoon white vinegar or rubbing alcohol

Baking sheet lined with paper towels

Paper plates

School glue

Place the dried pasta in the container. Add a few drops of food coloring and the vinegar or rubbing alcohol. Cover with the lid and shake.

Add more food coloring if needed and shake until the color is evenly distributed.

Pour the pasta on the baking sheet lined with a paper towel and let the pieces dry completely.

Once dry, use the pasta for crafts or sensory work for younger children. For example, create art by gluing the colored pasta to a plain paper plate using school glue.

Tips

- You can also color the pasta with acrylic paint instead of food coloring and vinegar or rubbing alcohol. Shake the pasta and paint in a plastic bag, then follow the remaining steps.
- The vinegar or rubbing alcohol will dissipate, so don't worry about dealing with a liquid mess!
- Store leftover colored pasta in a container and use for other crafts.

PASTA JEWELRY BOX

MAKES 1 BOX

Hot-glue gun

A few handfuls of a variety of dry pasta

Wood box

Spray paint

Use the hot glue to attach a variety of pasta to a wood box.

Take the box outside and spray-paint it with the desired color.

Allow the paint to dry completely before using the box.

Tips

- Make sure to spray-paint in a well-ventilated area, with at least 8 inches between you and the project.
- For added dimension, use a variety of dry pasta shapes.
- Keep in mind how the box opens and closes, so once the pasta is glued on, the box can still function properly.

CLAY TILE ART WITH PASTA

MAKES 1 TILE

Craft rolling pin

Clay

Variety of dry pasta

Roll out the clay to about $\frac{1}{4}$ inch thick.

Use the pasta to create different designs and shapes in the clay.

Tips

- You can use either nontoxic air-dry clay or oven-bake clay. Regardless, make sure to wash your hands after handling the clay.
- If you make the tiles similar shapes, you can create wall art with the finished product. This could be a fun ongoing project that you continuously add to.

GRANDPA FRANK'S CLASSIC SPAGHETTI AND MEATBALLS

Pretty much every Italian will tell you that their family has their own recipe for tomato sauce, and this recipe is mine. Even though the Provenzano side of my family sold J&R Sauce at the store, this is the recipe my grandpa would make at home for his family. The ingredients in this recipe were too expensive for them to mass-produce at the time, but it was perfect for Pasta Wednesday with the family.

When I make this recipe, it smells and tastes like my childhood and instantly transports me to my grandpa's house. I cry every time I cook it because it reminds me of him, and that is the power of food creating lasting memories! (photo page 34)

TOMATO SAUCE

MAKES 10 TO 15 SERVINGS

1/4 cup olive oil

1 large onion, finely chopped

1 tablespoon salt, plus extra for salting the oil and the water

4 cloves garlic, minced

28 ounces plum tomatoes, crushed

4 (12-ounce) cans tomato paste; for every can add three cans full of water

1/4 cup sugar

1 tablespoon salt, plus extra

1 teaspoon black pepper

1 Italian sausage, cooked

40 to 45 meatballs (page 43)

2 tablespoons fresh basil

2 to 3 inches of a Parmesan cheese rind, optional

1/2 cup freshly grated Parmesan cheese

2 pounds dried pasta

Heat the oil in a large pot. Add the onions and a sprinkle of salt. Cook over medium heat until the onions soften. Add the garlic and sauté for about 30 seconds, making sure not to overcook.

Add the tomatoes, tomato paste, water, sugar, salt, and pepper. It helps to whisk the tomato paste to break it up. Stir until the tomato paste becomes smooth.

Stir in the sausage, meatballs, basil, and Parmesan cheese rind (if using).

Simmer the sauce for about 4 hours. Adjust spices as needed. Stir in the Parmesan cheese.

Bring a large pot of water to a boil and add in enough salt to flavor the water. Add the pasta to the salted water and cook until al dente, being careful not to overcook.

Drain the pasta and put it back into the pot that it cooked in. Add enough sauce to saturate the pasta, about 4 cups or so, and let the pasta cook in the sauce for a few minutes.

To serve a crowd, pour the pasta into a large bowl and cover with more sauce and some of the meatballs. (This recipe makes a lot, so you may need two large bowls.) We always serve the extra meatballs and sauce on the side in a separate bowl, as well as extra Parmesan cheese for topping.

MEATBALLS

MAKES 40 TO 45 MEATBALLS

2 slices white bread, crust removed

½ cup whole milk

½ cup soft bread crumbs (about 2
slices of white bread, crusts removed)

1 ½ pounds ground pork

1 pound ground beef

½ teaspoon ground black pepper

½ teaspoon salt

2 to 4 tablespoons chopped
parsley (add as much or as
little as you like! I love parsley
so I like to add a little more)

½ cup freshly grated Parmesan cheese

2 large eggs, room temperature

4 cloves garlic, minced

If baking the meatballs, preheat the oven to 375 degrees.

In a small bowl, soak 2 slices of white bread in the milk.

Make soft bread crumbs by putting 2 slices of white bread (the amount may vary based on slice size) in a food processor and pulsing until the bread crumbles.

Combine the soaked bread slices, soft bread crumbs, ground pork, ground beef, pepper, salt, parsley, Parmesan cheese, eggs, and garlic in a large bowl and mix together with two forks. Use your hands to make sure all ingredients are well incorporated into the mixture, but do not overmix.

Use a cookie scoop to scoop out the meatballs. This is the easiest way to make sure they're all the same size and cook evenly. Use your hands to shape the scooped mixture into a smooth meatball.

Place the meatballs on a baking sheet lined with aluminum foil and bake for about 15 minutes, or fry in a pan for 10 to 15 minutes, browning on all sides. They'll continue to cook in the sauce as it simmers.

Add the meatballs to the sauce.

Tips

- Adding sugar to the sauce won't make it sweet. The touch of sweetness helps balance out the sauce.
- Don't skip the Italian sausage. Even though it's only one link, it makes a huge difference in taste.
- Adding a Parmesan cheese rind to the pasta sauce is an Italian secret. It isn't even written in my grandpa's recipe. I just know from years of having his sauce—and my mom's sauce—that it's hidden in there. You don't have to include it, but it infuses a delicious, subtle Parmesan flavor.
- My grandpa liked to strain the sauce because it seemed more professional to him. To strain, remove the meatballs, then pour the sauce through a sieve into another pot, using a spatula to push the sauce through. It helps to strain half the sauce, clean the sieve, and then strain the other half. You can use an immersion blender to make the sauce smooth.

LEMONY SHRIMP WITH BUCATINI

Even though this dish sounds fancy, it's super easy. The key is to let the pasta cook in the sauce for a bit. The lemon infuses into the pasta, and the flavors marry perfectly. I can't get enough of the lemon flavor, so I like to finish off the dish with freshly squeezed lemon juice.

MAKES 4 SERVINGS

1 pound medium-size shrimp, peeled, deveined, and tails removed

1 pound bucatini pasta

Salt and pepper to taste

2 tablespoons unsalted butter

3 to 4 tablespoons olive oil

1 garlic clove, minced

1/4 teaspoon crushed red pepper flakes, optional

1 to 2 teaspoons fresh lemon zest (about the zest of one lemon)

1/2 cup freshly squeezed lemon juice, plus more to taste

1/2 cup Parmesan cheese, freshly grated, divided

1/2 cup fresh parsley

While you prep the shrimp, boil the pasta in a large pot of salted water until al dente (that is, not overcooked).

Rinse and dry the shrimp, then lightly sprinkle the shrimp with salt and pepper.

Heat the butter and oil in a large skillet over medium to medium-high heat. Add the shrimp and cook on one side for a couple of minutes. Flip the shrimp to cook the other side.

Add the garlic and crushed red pepper and cook for about 30 seconds, being careful not to let the garlic brown or it will taste bitter. Add the lemon zest and juice and stir.

Use tongs to grab the bucatini out of the pot and place it directly into the pan with the shrimp. Before stirring, pour 1/4 cup of the Parmesan cheese over the pasta. Toss everything well and allow the pasta to cook in the sauce for a few minutes.

Add the fresh parsley and toss to combine. Add salt, pepper, lemon juice, and the remaining Parmesan cheese to taste. Add a few tablespoons of pasta water while stirring everything together.

Tips

- Buy high-quality shrimp, and ask for it to be peeled and deveined so you don't have to do that yourself.
- If you don't have bucatini, classic spaghetti is a perfect alternative.
- Adding the Parmesan cheese to the pasta before tossing it with the sauce helps the pasta hold on to the sauce better.
- I like to add veggies, such as green beans, asparagus, or zucchini. Sauté them in a separate skillet until al dente (that is, not overcooked), then cook them with the pasta in the sauce so the veggies soak up that glorious lemon and garlic flavor.

HOW TO MAKE PASTA FROM SCRATCH

Making homemade pasta isn't as difficult as it seems. The biggest problem is that the ingredients are rarely exact. Everyone who makes homemade pasta regularly will tell you: it's all about feel. You know when you've added enough flour; you know when you've kneaded the pasta enough. With practice, you will know! Almost every Italian has a different way of making homemade pasta, and there's no right or wrong way. This is simply my way.

MAKES 4 TO 6 SERVINGS

4 or 5 large eggs, room temperature

Pinch of salt

2 tablespoons olive oil

3 to 4 cups 00 flour, plus more for rolling out

Place 4 eggs, salt, and olive oil in a food processor and pulse to mix together, about 5 to 10 seconds. Scoop 3 cups of flour into the food processor and process until it starts to form a ball. If it's too wet, add more flour. If it doesn't come together and is crumbly, add another egg.

Remove the dough from the food processor and place it on a clean countertop. Knead the dough, adding a bit more flour if the dough is too sticky. Knead for another minute or two, until the dough is smooth.

Let the dough sit at room temperature for about 20 minutes, or put it in the fridge to roll out at a later time. (If the dough has been chilled, bring it to room temperature before using.)

To roll out the dough, cut it into quarters. Use your hands to flatten one of the pieces, adding a couple tablespoons of flour if needed.

Use a pasta roller/cutter to flatten the dough until you can see through it. Machines vary, so start at a thicker setting and work your way down to a thinner setting before cutting. Then feed the pasta through the cutter to get the size noodles you want.

Toss the cut pasta with a couple more tablespoons of flour so it doesn't stick together.

Flatten and cut the rest of the dough piece by piece. At this point, you can either cook the pasta or freeze it.

Cook the pasta in salted boiling water for 3 to 5 minutes or until cooked through. After the pasta is cooked, add it to any sauce recipe you like.

Tips for Making and Cooking Pasta

- Using 00 flour will give you pasta that is light and airy but also has a good bite. You can use all-purpose flour, but the pasta will be denser.
- To make pasta without the food processor, place the flour on a clean countertop and create a well in the center. Pour all the ingredients into the well. Use a fork to whisk the wet ingredients, slowly incorporating the dry. When I use this method, I tend to need more flour than for the food processor method.
- If you don't have a pasta roller/cutter, you can use a rolling pin and cut the pasta with a knife. If you roll out the dough, be sure to make it very thin.
- Pasta freezes beautifully. Store in freezer-safe sandwich bags for up to one month.
- Instead of pouring the sauce over the pasta, let the pasta cook in the sauce. Hot pasta better absorbs the sauce and allows the flavors to marry.
- Salt the water! This adds wonderful flavor to the pasta, even if you want to eat it plain with butter, which we do in our house all the time. I usually add a palmful, but that can mean different things to different people. So how much salt to use? Start with a pinch of salt, grab a wooden spoon, and taste the water. If it tastes like water, then you need more salt; if it tastes like the ocean, you added too much. You'll figure out what is right for you.

Tips: **Punch Up the Flavor with Pesto**

Pesto is an easy way to add tons of flavor to a variety of dishes, and it's simple enough for beginners and experts alike to master in minutes. Pair it with a protein or a carb, and you'll never get bored of your lunch or dinner. You can freeze pesto by scooping it into ice cube trays, then popping out the cubes and storing them in a freezer-safe container labeled with the date. It will keep in the freezer for up to six months. This way, you can use one or two cubes at a time instead of having to thaw out the entire batch. Presto! Or should I say, *pesto!* You've got a mouthwatering meal in minutes. (photo page 52)

LEMONY BASIL PESTO

MAKES ABOUT 1 CUP

1/2 cup pine nuts

1/2 cup freshly grated Parmesan cheese

3 heaping cups fresh basil

1 teaspoon fresh lemon zest

2 to 3 tablespoons freshly squeezed lemon juice

2 garlic cloves, peeled

1/4 cup extra-virgin olive oil

Salt and pepper to taste

Place the pine nuts in a shallow skillet over medium heat, tossing and stirring frequently. Toast until the nuts are fragrant and slightly brown. Be careful—this can happen quickly! Allow the pine nuts to cool.

Place the cooled pine nuts, Parmesan cheese, basil, lemon zest, lemon juice, and garlic cloves into a food processor. Process all of the ingredients together for about 15 seconds.

With the mixer running slowly, pour in the olive oil.

Add salt and pepper to taste. Process again to mix. If the pesto is too thick, add more olive oil.

Store in the refrigerator in a sealed container for up to 5 days.

PUMPKIN SEED PESTO

MAKES ABOUT 1 1/2 CUPS

3 cups raw hulled pumpkin seeds (pepitas)

2 garlic cloves, peeled

1 cup fresh flat-leaf parsley

1 to 2 teaspoons ground chili pepper (I like ancho chili)

1 heaping teaspoon ground cinnamon

2 tablespoons freshly squeezed lemon juice

3/4 cup extra-virgin olive oil

Salt and pepper to taste

Preheat the oven to 350 degrees.

Line a baking sheet with aluminum foil. Place the pumpkin seeds on the baking sheet. Bake until fragrant and slightly starting to brown, about 5 to 10 minutes. Set aside to cool.

Place the garlic in the food processor and process until the pieces are fine. Add the pumpkin seeds, parsley, chili pepper, and cinnamon. Pulse to combine.

With the processor running slowly, add the lemon juice and olive oil in a steady stream until combined.

Season with salt and pepper.

Store in the refrigerator in an airtight container for up to 5 days.

This is a thicker pesto. It can be thinned out to make it drizzle better by adding more olive oil.

ROASTED RED PEPPER PESTO

MAKES ABOUT 2 CUPS

1 cup toasted pine nuts

3/4 cup whole milk ricotta cheese

1 cup jarred roasted red peppers

1/2 cup freshly grated pecorino

2 teaspoons fresh oregano

1/2 cup fresh basil leaves

2 tablespoons freshly squeezed lemon juice

1/2 cup extra-virgin olive oil

Salt and pepper to taste

Place the pine nuts in a shallow skillet over medium heat, tossing and stirring frequently. Toast until the nuts are fragrant and slightly brown. Careful—this won't take long! Remove the nuts from the skillet and allow them to cool.

Once cool, place the pine nuts, ricotta, roasted red peppers, pecorino, oregano, basil, and lemon juice into a food processor or blender. Process everything together.

With the processor running, gradually add the olive oil through the opening in the lid. Add more olive oil as needed until you reach the desired consistency.

Taste for flavor and add more herbs and salt and pepper if needed.

TAKEOUT
THURSDAY

Grab your phone, open that to-go app, snatch those takeout menus that are constantly cluttering up your drawers, and embrace the fun of Takeout Thursday! Whether it's your favorite Chinese restaurant, an Italian eatery, or all-American fare, reinvent the typical delivery night experience by adding DIYs and a few of my favorite tips to upgrade your to-go cuisine.

This is one of my favorite nights because it's a night off from cooking, but it's also a great opportunity to support local restaurant owners and their staff. Back when I worked at a restaurant, one of my unforgettable memories was forming bonds with our regular customers. Now that I can show support for my local restaurants and eateries, being their regular customer warms my heart. Forming relationships with these restaurants builds community and brings people together.

You can even make it a date night. After so many years together, my husband and I still swear by our regular date nights. Every other week, we look forward to using Thursday evenings as a night to get a sitter and unwind, treat ourselves, and reconnect. So get creative and connect with your partner while also supporting a local eatery in your neighborhood.

Let your kids pick their favorite local restaurant for a takeout meal they can eat while you're out for the evening. That will keep them excited about the special weekly dinner routine.

---

* Sponsored product; see author's note on page ix.

Take out Thursday!

Tonight's Menu:

Fried Rice
+
Orange chicken

DRY-ERASE PLACE MAT

Get your little ones excited about their takeout food by setting the table in the morning with this DIY Dry-Erase Place Mat! They can write their orders before they leave for the day and look forward to their order being delivered for dinner. This also is a fun way to sneak in a lesson about the alphabet or some arithmetic without your kids knowing. An added bonus for parents is that the kids can doodle away on their place mats during dinner, so you may be able to have a real conversation with each other.

MAKES 1 PLACE MAT

Marker or paint pen

Paper

Colored tape (optional)

Scissors

Dry-erase markers

Self-seal laminating sheets

Use the marker or paint pen to write a name, phrase, and/or design at the top of the paper.

Apply strips of tape and create lines for the kids to write on (optional).

Seal the paper with the self-seal laminating sheets. The laminate will allow the kids to draw, erase, and redraw over and over with dry-erase markers!

Tips

- You can teach your kids how to set their place setting by drawing the setting right on the place mat as a template for them to follow.
- Allow your kids to make their own place mats so they're excited to use them each week.
- Change up the place mats seasonally.
- Have a local print shop hard laminate your place mats if desired.

SEASONAL COCKTAILS

I love pairing takeout with a quality cocktail from scratch. It feels like stepping out when you're really only stepping to your table—my kind of commute.

SPRING: APEROL SPRITZ

This classic Italian *aperitivo* never goes out of style. Channel your Sophia Loren vibes as you sip this classy cocktail. The floral notes of Aperol pair perfectly with the lovely, light sweetness of the prosecco, a splash of club soda, and a garnish of an orange wedge. You'll feel like you're being whisked away on a Vespa through the cobblestone streets of Tuscany.

MAKES 1 DRINK

Ice

3 ounces La Gioiosa Prosecco DOC*

2 ounces Aperol

2 ounces club soda or sparkling water

Orange slices for garnish

Mint sprig or basil for garnish, optional

Fill a large wine glass with ice.

Add the prosecco, Aperol, and club soda or sparkling water. Stir gently to combine.

Garnish with the orange slice and mint or basil (if desired).

Tips

- Classic Aperol spritz recipes use less soda water, but I add a touch more so it's nice and bubbly.
- Make sure not to stir too much or you'll lose the bubbles.
- Don't use flat prosecco! After opening, use a stopper to preserve the bubbles.

---

* Sponsored product; see author's note on page ix.

SUMMER: SPICY GRAPEFRUIT JALAPEÑO MARGARITA

You can't go wrong with a classic marg, but I like to change it up a bit and make it extra pretty. This unique recipe is salty, sweet, tart, and slightly spicy, but also refreshing. This is the drink to have as you kick off your shoes and watch the sunset.

MAKES A PITCHER
(APPROXIMATELY 8 DRINKS)

1 1/4 cup tequila

2 cups freshly squeezed grapefruit juice

1 cup fresh lime juice

4 tablespoons honey or agave nectar

1 to 2 whole jalapeño peppers, sliced

1 tablespoon chili powder

3 teaspoons sugar

1 tablespoon kosher salt

Ice

Grapefruit, lime, and jalapeño
pepper slices for garnish

Mix the tequila, grapefruit juice, lime juice, honey, and jalapeños in a pitcher and stir well to combine.

Refrigerate for 30 minutes to 2 hours, checking spiciness from time to time, and remove the jalapeños from the pitcher when the desired spiciness is reached.

In a small bowl, combine the chili powder, sugar, and salt. Pour the mixture into a shallow dish. When ready to serve, rub a lime around the rim of each glass and then dip the rims into the spice mixture.

Add ice cubes to each glass and pour in the margarita mixture. Garnish with a grapefruit wedge, a lime wedge, and jalapeño slices.

Tips

- Use oranges instead of grapefruit for a slightly sweeter drink.
- To serve your drinks in chilled glasses, rinse the glasses under water and pop them into the freezer for about 15 minutes before pouring.

FALL: SPIKED HOT APPLE CIDER

I love fall! Maybe it's the midwesterner in me, but the crispness of the air, breaking out my favorite sweaters, and the coziness of it all makes me nostalgic and happy. Pour yourself a piping cup of Spiked Hot Apple Cider and breathe in the cinnamon aromas as the days get shorter and the mercury dips in the thermometer. This drink is comfy in a mug!

MAKES 8 TO 10 SERVINGS

1/2 gallon apple cider

2 cinnamon sticks, plus more for garnish

1 teaspoon whole cloves

1/4 cup fresh orange juice

1 tablespoon freshly grated orange zest

1 teaspoon grated ginger (or more to taste)

1/2 cup spiced rum or brandy (or to taste)

Thin apple slices for garnish

Put the apple cider, cinnamon sticks, cloves, orange juice, orange zest, and ginger into a saucepan and bring to a boil. Reduce to a simmer and cook on low for about 10 to 15 minutes.

Remove from the heat and drain in a fine-mesh colander to remove the spices.

Stir in the rum. Add extra cinnamon sticks and thinly sliced apple for a garnish. Serve warm.

Tips

- Keep the cider warm in the slow cooker, and serve the alcohol on the side instead of stirring it in. This is great for get-togethers and for designated drivers who might want to partake of the cider but not the alcohol.
- This recipe can easily be doubled if serving a crowd.

WINTER: EGGNOG YOU WILL ACTUALLY LIKE WITH SUGARED ROSEMARY SPRIGS

Eggnog is a classic during the holiday season, but truth be told, I don't usually like it. The thought of raw eggs doesn't sound too appetizing to me! I found a solution by cooking the eggs and creating a creamy mixture that tastes like crème anglaise. If you don't like eggnog, try this recipe! This concoction is a crowd-pleaser when we raise our glasses to wish health, happiness, and good cheer to one and all!

MAKES 8 TO 10 SERVINGS

12 eggs

1 cup sugar

4 cups whole milk

1/2 teaspoon nutmeg

1/2 teaspoon cinnamon

1/4 teaspoon salt

1 cup heavy whipping cream, room temperature

1 teaspoon vanilla extract

Spiced rum, to taste (bourbon works too)

TOPPINGS

1 cup heavy whipping cream

Fresh nutmeg

Fresh orange zest

Whisk the eggs and sugar in a bowl until thoroughly combined.

Pour the milk into a saucepan and stir in the nutmeg, cinnamon, and salt. Whisk the egg mixture into the milk mixture.

Heat the mixture over medium heat while stirring constantly. Use a candy thermometer to monitor the mixture's temperature. When it reaches 165 degrees, remove the pot from the heat and whisk in the heavy whipping cream and vanilla extract. Cool slightly before tasting and add more sugar or spices as desired.

Once cooled, pour the mixture into a covered container and refrigerate overnight or until thoroughly chilled.

Before serving, blend the mixture for a few seconds until frothy and light. Add the rum (if desired).

Make the whipped topping: In a chilled, medium bowl beat the heavy whipping cream with a hand mixer until soft peaks form.

Top each cup with whipped topping, nutmeg, and orange zest, and serve.

Tips

- Stirring constantly is very important to prevent the milk from scorching and the eggs from scrambling.
- If you do not have a large blender on hand, an immersion blender works as well.
- Start with a half cup of rum and then add more until you achieve the taste you like. You can also serve the alcohol on the side so guests can add as much as they like.
- If serving in a punch bowl, either fold the fresh whipped cream into the mixture for a traditional look or keep it separate and use it as a topping made to order.

SUGARED ROSEMARY SPRIG

MAKES 8 TO 10 SPRIGS

½ cup sugar

½ cup water

8 to 10 fresh rosemary sprigs

1 heaping cup granulated, cane, or sparkling sugar for coating

Place the sugar and water in a small saucepan over medium-high heat. Stir until the sugar dissolves and the mixture begins to boil.

Remove from heat. Add the rosemary sprigs and steep for 4 to 5 minutes.

Using a slotted spoon, remove the rosemary from the saucepan and place it on a baking rack or parchment paper for about 10 minutes.

Place 1 heaping cup of granulated, cane, or sparkling sugar in a small bowl. Add a rosemary sprig, using your fingers or a small spoon to gently roll it in the sugar to coat completely. Place the sprig on a clean baking rack to dry. Repeat with the remaining rosemary sprigs.

Allow the sprigs to dry at room temperature for one hour.

Tips: Upgrade Your Takeout

- **Incorporate fresh herbs.** Add hardy herbs like thyme, rosemary, oregano, and sage to your next takeout dish to maximize the flavor and make an ordinary to-go meal sing!
- **Plate it.** Restaurants typically ensure their food is plated properly, so take note. The thoughtful presentation can make a simple meal feel extravagant simply by adding it to a plate. We eat with all of our senses: what we see, smell, and feel makes a difference. Use this opportunity to add personality to your takeout by choosing the right vessel when presenting your dish.
- **Add some music.** A well-chosen tune can set a cheerful mood around the dinner table, and it's the perfect opportunity to get the kids involved. Ask them to help you pick out a song or even create a family playlist.
- **Don't forget the drinks.** Pairing your food with a specialty cocktail or mocktail can make an average meal feel extra special.

THE BEST FOODS FOR TAKEOUT

Too busy to cook? These are my tastiest choices that travel well.

- **Pizza:** I think we can all agree that the number one takeout food is pizza. It's hard to say why it universally brings us all together, but basically everyone can go for bread and cheese! I suggest opting for a local pizzeria for your delivery order rather than one of the chains. You get fresh ingredients, plus you support a local business.
- **A burrito bowl:** I'll let you in on my secret to-go order: whenever I'm craving Mexican food, I opt for ordering a piled-high burrito bowl instead of a traditional burrito. It travels better, and your tortilla doesn't get soggy and ruined. Create your own burrito with a tortilla from home, or serve these bowls with fresh, crunchy chips, and your Mexican-food craving will be easily satisfied.
- **Chicken tenders:** Not only is this meal pretty much my children's favorite, but it travels so well. The white meat pieces always end up arriving with more integrity than my salad or sandwich orders. So channel your childhood and order some tasty tenders!
- **Instant-comfort soup:** When all you want is a blanket and a warm, cozy fire, opt for ordering soup. It travels well and is simple to reheat. No matter the cuisine you're craving—Thai, Italian, Greek, Mexican, you name it—it offers a soup option.

---

* Sponsored product; see author's note on page ix.

FRIDAY FETE

Hooray—it's FriYAY! You made it through the week, and that's cause for celebration. Give yourself a hearty pat on the back for a job well done (or, depending on how the week turned out, a job done). Maybe you're kicking off your end-of-week victory with the family or a gathering with a few of your friends, so naturally, you want to make it feel like a real celebration. I've always thought adding little touches to the everyday turns mundane moments into extraordinary memories. This chapter is designed to inspire you to celebrate today with ease, instead of waiting for a holiday or big event.

Set the Scene

Let's dive right into the spirit of celebration. I say it's time to bring out the good stuff. Yes, I'm serious. We wait until the holidays to use our fancy plates, but life is too short to use those gorgeous items only once a year. And when it comes to stemware, who said you can only use the good champagne glasses for New Year's Eve? Break out those fine champagne flutes and share a toast with your favorite people. Creating a party in your own home on a random Friday by adding a touch of "fancy" will make the whole night feel extra special. Cheers!

---

*   Sponsored product; see author's note on page ix.

THREE WAYS TO MAKE HOMEMADE CONFETTI

Recycle: Use a hole punch and paper you're planning to dispose of to create tiny circles.

Chop chop: All you need is a pair of scissors and some tissue paper, and you're in business. Simply cut the tissue paper into strips and celebrate!

Flower power: Pluck the petals off your flowers and place them onto a rimmed baking sheet lined with parchment paper. Then bake at 200 degrees for about 10 minutes, until they're dry and crispy. After your petals are dry, you can put them all in a basket until you're ready to use them. Make sure not to get the floral confetti wet as the colors from the flowers can bleed.

CREAMY TUSCAN SALMON

Don't let the "Tuscan" intimidate you. This is a simple dish to prepare and one I'm sure you'll revisit again and again. Full of traditional flavors like olive oil, sun-dried tomato, and garlic, this recipe is quick but luxurious and has a sophisticated feel to it. The rich salmon and creamy sauce pair well with a glass of bubbly (*hint hint*). (photo page 73)

MAKES 4 SERVINGS

4 (8-ounce) salmon fillets

1/2 teaspoon salt, divided

1 tablespoon olive oil

2 tablespoons unsalted butter

1 large (or two small) shallot, diced

3 cloves garlic, minced

1/2 cup jarred sun-dried tomatoes in oil, drained

1/4 cup vegetable broth

1/4 cup white wine

3/4 cup heavy cream, room temperature

Pepper to taste

2 cups baby spinach leaves

1/4 cup freshly grated Parmesan cheese

1/4 cup chopped fresh parsley

Pat the salmon dry with a paper towel and season the fillets with 1/4 to 1/2 teaspoon salt.

Heat the oil in a large skillet over medium-high heat. Sear the salmon, flesh-side down first, for 4 minutes on each side or until cooked to your liking. After the fillets are cooked, remove them from the pan and set aside.

In the same pan, melt the butter. Add the shallot and cook until translucent. Add the garlic and sauté until fragrant, about 30 seconds. Add the sun-dried tomatoes and let them cook for 1 to 2 minutes, so they release their flavors.

Stir in the vegetable broth and white wine, and allow the sauce to reduce down for about 5 minutes. Reduce the heat to low and stir in the heavy cream.

Bring the sauce to a gentle simmer while stirring occasionally. Season with the remaining 1/4 teaspoon of salt and pepper to taste. Stir in the baby spinach and allow it to wilt in the sauce. Tongs work well for this. Stir in the Parmesan cheese and let the cream sauce simmer for another minute to allow the cheese to melt.

Place the grilled salmon fillets back in the pan. Sprinkle with the parsley, and spoon the sauce over each fillet. Serve hot.

Tips

- The salmon can be replaced with chicken. Pound the chicken so it isn't too thick, which will help it cook evenly and quickly.
- The skin helps the salmon fillets retain their shape while you sear them and protects them from over-cooking. If you want to remove the skin before adding the fillets back to the pan, slide a fork between the salmon fillet and the skin. It's much easier to remove the skin after the salmon is cooked.
- Season the salmon with salt right before searing. If you do this too far in advance, the salt will pull out moisture and prevent the salmon from getting nicely seared. If you salt the fillets too soon, don't worry. Just pat them dry with a paper towel.
- Searing the salmon flesh-side down first (skin-side up) creates a nice crust over the top of the salmon. To get a great sear, make sure the skillet is hot and the olive oil rolls easily around the skillet, but be careful that it's not hot enough to burn.
- The key to a perfectly creamy sauce is to gently simmer it to avoid separating and curdling the cream.
- I like a lot of sauce, so I tend to double the recipe so I can dip bread in it.

LEMONY FENNEL AND ARUGULA SALAD WITH PINE NUTS

I love serving a bright and refreshing salad alongside a rich, decadent dish. This salad is a great staple to have in your back pocket because it's simple yet anything but boring. It can be turned into a main dish by topping it with grilled chicken, shrimp, or other protein.

MAKES 4 SERVINGS

5 to 6 heaping cups of arugula

½ cup pine nuts, toasted (see step 1 on page 51)

1 fennel bulb, thinly sliced

Sourdough Croutons (page 75)

Lemony Salad Dressing (page 75)

Sea salt and freshly ground black pepper to taste

Wash and dry the arugula and place onto a large platter. Top with the pine nuts, fennel, and the Sourdough Croutons. Drizzle the Lemony Salad Dressing over the salad, adding as much as you like. Season with sea salt and black pepper to taste.

Tips

- Toast the pine nuts by placing them in a small skillet over medium heat. Cook until they start to become fragrant and slightly golden, stirring constantly to prevent them from burning.
- Slice the fennel with a mandoline. Be sure to remove the core of the fennel bulb since it is too tough to eat.
- I like serving salads on large platters instead of in bowls. It's a better way to distribute the toppings evenly, and the heavy ingredients don't get lost in the bottom of the bowl.

SOURDOUGH CROUTONS

MAKES 4 CUPS

1 loaf sourdough bread (about
4 cups cubed bread)

2 tablespoons butter

1 garlic clove, minced

1 tablespoons olive oil

1/2 teaspoon kosher salt

1/4 cup freshly chopped flat-leaf parsley

Cut sourdough bread into 1-inch cubes and place in a large bowl.

Place the butter into a small skillet over medium heat. Once it's melted, add in the garlic and cook, swirling it around in the skillet, until it becomes fragrant, about 30 seconds.

Pour the butter mixture and the olive oil over the bread. Sprinkle with salt and use your hands or a spatula to toss everything together until the bread is evenly coated.

Line a rimmed baking sheet with parchment paper. Add the bread into the pan in an even layer.

Bake at 350 degrees for 15 to 20 minutes or until golden and crisp, turning over croutons halfway through.

LEMONY SALAD DRESSING

MAKES ABOUT 1 1/2 CUPS

7 tablespoons freshly
squeezed lemon juice

1 tablespoon Dijon mustard

1 garlic clove, minced

1 teaspoon salt

1/2 teaspoon ground black pepper

1 cup olive oil

Basil or parsley to taste, optional

Combine the lemon juice, Dijon mustard, garlic, salt, and pepper in a blender.

Slowly add in the olive oil.

Adjust seasonings to taste. Add in fresh herbs, such as basil or parsley, for additional flavor.

This can also be mixed up in a mason jar and shaken until combined.

CHOCOLATE MOUSSE WITH COOKIE CRUMBLE TOPPING

This chocolate mousse with cookie crumble topping is almost too good for words—*almost*. This dessert is always a hit on Valentine's Day, but why not bring some of that romantic spirit to your life on a random Friday? Share this sinfully delicious confection with your special someone, or treat yourself to this mousse goodness. You're worth it!

MAKES ABOUT 5 CUPS
(6 TO 8 SERVINGS)

8 ounces semisweet chocolate chips

1/2 cup coffee

2 tablespoons unsweetened Dutch-processed cocoa

1 tablespoon firmly packed brown sugar

1/2 teaspoon kosher salt

1 1/2 cups heavy whipping cream

2 teaspoons vanilla extract

6 to 8 Classic Chocolate Chip Cookies (page 215)

In a large mixing bowl, combine the chocolate chips, coffee, cocoa, brown sugar, and salt. Place over a pot of simmering water to create a double boiler. Stir until the mixture is smooth and well combined. Set aside to cool.

In the bowl of a stand mixer with a whisk attachment, whisk the heavy whipping cream until it forms stiff peaks. This can also be done in a large bowl with a hand mixer. Fold the whipped cream and vanilla extract into the chocolate mixture.

Divide the mixture evenly between 6 to 8 dessert glasses, cover, and chill in the refrigerator until set, for about 1 hour.

If using frozen cookies, remove them from the freezer while the mousse sets. Break them into small pieces once they're about room temperature. Sprinkle the chocolate chip cookie crumbles over the chocolate mousse and serve.

Tips

- If you need to avoid caffeine, substitute water for the coffee.
- Don't overwhisk the heaving whipping cream, or else it will become too lumpy.
- The mousse can be frozen in the individual cups as long as they are covered. Or store it in a freezer-safe container for up to two months, and scoop to serve.
- This recipe also pairs well with fresh-baked Classic Chocolate Chip Cookies (page 215)!
- For a dairy-free mousse, use dairy-free chocolate chips and substitute coconut milk for the heavy cream.

Tips: **Spruce Up Your Spritz**

A glass of bubbly always feels like a mini celebration, even if the only thing you're celebrating is the fact that you survived the work week. This is why I always have La Gioiosa Prosecco in the fridge.* Pop open a bottle of this prosecco any day of the week for an instant party. To make those moments even more special, a little crafty touch can make a big impact.

Chill in style. I'm a huge advocate of waste not, want not. I love having fresh flowers around, and instead of tossing them out when they start to wilt, I like to repurpose them into the prettiest ice bucket you'll ever see. Simply add the flowers to an ice cube tray, fill with water, and then freeze. When you're ready for a Friday Fete, fill your ice bucket with these beautiful flower ice cubes to chill your bubbly.

Make her fancy. You also can add confetti to your wine glasses with a coat of Mod Podge, being sure to only add the confetti to the center of the glass and below; avoid applying adhesive to the rim of the glass. (photo page 66)

Turn it into a treat. Add a scoop of sorbet (I like raspberry or lemon) to your champagne glass and top it off with some bubbly. (photo page 69)

---

*   Sponsored product; see author's note on page ix.

WONDERFULLY
SWEET
WEEKEND

Ah, the weekend. The special forty-eight hours that make us feel oh-so-happy. You've put in five days of hard work, so why not give yourself a bit of a break with some revelry for your Saturday and Sunday? Weekends are made to be special and to experience a calmer, gentler pace. Our schedules can get pretty hectic, so let the weekends give you that excuse to reset and relax, at least the best you can. In our house, we love to make something sweet for breakfast on the weekend. A kitchen that is humming with activity and smells like fresh scones or muffins will have those late sleepers in your house rubbing their eyes and moseying their way out of their slumber to find a spot at the table in no time. With a few special recipes and some added touches, you'll be wiping crumbs off happy faces!

Set the Scene

Weekends are all about cozy comfort! Even if the weekends are packed with soccer games, trips to the farmers market, and so much more, I think there's no time like the present to take a beat on the weekend to stay in your pj's, embrace your bed head, savor that cup of coffee, and spend some quiet time with family. Ambiance is everything, so I always do my best to create a hygge feel to make the most of the morning. Here are some of my favorite strategies:

- Play a soothing playlist like "Coffee Shop Music" or "Sunday Chill" on Spotify.
- The most satisfying presentation has a deeper meaning. That's why I love to mix and match vintage plates or use the flowery teacup set my mom gave me for a sweet, idyllic feel; pair these things with linen napkins and modern cutlery for an eclectic vibe.
- Add some freshly cut (or freshly purchased) flowers to an unconventional vase like a pitcher or vintage bowl for a romantic but relaxed feel.

WOODEN CLIPBOARD WALL ORGANIZERS AND FRAMES

I love when DIY meets function. From homework to artwork, there is almost always a tornado of papers heading my way. As always, my solution involves a little crafting. These clipboards are so simple to make but also easy to customize to fit the aesthetic of your home. This DIY project will make you feel less overwhelmed and will help you conquer that paper pile once and for all.

MAKES 1 CLIPBOARD

Sandpaper, optional

Wood rectangle for crafts

Wood stain and rags, optional

Ruler

Pencil

Wood glue or superglue

2 wood clothespins or clips

Wood sealer, optional

Mounting tape

Use the sandpaper to buff out the sharp edges on the wood rectangle, if needed.

Stain the wood by dipping the rag in the stain and rubbing it onto the wood until evenly covered. Be sure not to over-saturate the wood. Use another dry rag to wipe excess stain off. Allow the wood to dry completely.

Use a ruler to measure out the space for the clothespins so they are placed evenly on both the right and left side of the board, then lightly mark the spaces with a pencil.

Use the wood glue to attach the clothespins onto the premeasured marks. Allow the glue to dry completely. Seal the wood with a wood sealer, if desired.

Hang the clipboard on the wall with mounting tape.

 Tips

- The size and shape of the wood base can be adjusted to any space or aesthetic. It's also up to you if you want the edges to be rounded out by the sandpaper or to be left pointed.
- Let your kids decorate their own clipboards.
- Sealing these wood pieces is optional, but it's a good idea because it keeps the wood looking clean and prevents unwanted stains.

LEMON AND BLUEBERRY MUFFINS WITH LEMONY CRUMBLE

My household is obsessed with lemons. Maybe it's our Sicilian blood, but both my kids and I will add lemon to anything and everything. These muffins have a crunchy, crumbly, lemony topping, plus a burst of acidity from the blueberries, and they contain the perfect balance of sweet and tart flavors.

MAKES 14 TO 16 MUFFINS

¼ cup unsalted butter, room temperature

¼ cup coconut oil, room temperature (not melted)

1 cup sugar

1 cup sour cream, room temperature

2 teaspoons fresh lemon zest

¼ cup freshly squeezed lemon juice

1 teaspoon vanilla extract

2 cups plus 1 tablespoon all-purpose flour, divided

½ teaspoon baking powder

½ teaspoon baking soda

½ teaspoon salt

2 large eggs, room temperature

1 cup fresh blueberries

LEMONY CRUMBLE

¾ cup all-purpose flour

¾ cup sugar

¼ teaspoon salt

2 to 3 teaspoons fresh lemon zest (approximately one small lemon)

5 tablespoons unsalted butter, room temperature

Preheat the oven to 350 degrees.

In a stand mixer (or in a large bowl using a hand mixer) cream the butter, coconut oil, and sugar together until light and fluffy.

In a separate small bowl, mix together the sour cream, lemon zest, lemon juice, and vanilla extract.

In a medium bowl, mix together 2 cups of flour, baking powder, baking soda, and salt.

With the mixer running, add in the eggs one at a time and mix until incorporated. Add the flour mixture and the sour cream mixture, alternating by starting and finishing with the flour mixture. Don't overmix.

Toss the blueberries with 1 tablespoon flour and fold them into the muffin batter with a spatula.

Place muffin liners into a muffin pan, or spray the pan with cooking spray to bake the muffins without a liner (my preference is without a liner). Use a scoop to evenly distribute the batter into the prepared muffin pan.

Make the crumble by mixing the flour, sugar, salt, and lemon zest together. Stir in the butter.

Use your hands to knead the mixture until it resembles sand and sticks together when you squeeze it. Sprinkle the crumble generously over the muffins.

Bake at 350 degrees for about 25 minutes or until the muffins have puffed up and a toothpick comes out clean when inserted in the center of the muffin.

Allow them to cool just enough to handle before removing from the pan. The blueberries can stick to the pan if they cool too much in the pan. These are best served hot.

ITALIAN BREAKFAST CAKE

Leave it up to the Italians to have cake for breakfast. This breakfast cake, known to the Italians as *ciambella*, is light and lovely with a kiss of sweetness. The textures and flavors are very similar to those of a pound cake, but this one has a slight citrus flavor from either lemon or lime. This sweet treat is bound to be the absolute highlight of your morning.

MAKES 1 BUNDT CAKE

3 cups all-purpose flour

1 tablespoon baking powder

2 teaspoons freshly grated lemon zest

1/2 teaspoon kosher salt

3 large eggs, room temperature

1 1/4 cups sugar

3/4 cup olive oil

3/4 cup whole milk, room temperature

1/4 cup sour cream, room temperature

1/4 cup freshly squeezed lemon juice

1 teaspoon pure vanilla extract

1/2 cup apricot jelly or jam, optional

2 to 4 tablespoons powdered sugar

Preheat the oven to 350 degrees.

In a large bowl, whisk together the flour, baking powder, lemon zest, and salt, and set aside.

Add the eggs into the bowl of a stand mixer. (You can also use a large bowl and a hand mixer.) With the mixer on low, add the sugar. Beat the eggs and sugar on medium speed until light and fluffy and pale in color, about 2 to 3 minutes.

In a separate medium bowl, mix together the olive oil, milk, sour cream, lemon juice, and vanilla extract. With the mixer on medium-low, stir in the milk mixture until smooth and combined.

With the mixer on low, slowly add in the flour mixture and mix until combined, being careful not to overmix.

Spray the Bundt pan with cooking spray. Pour the batter into the prepared pan and bake for 40 to 50 minutes or until a toothpick inserted in the center comes out without any crumbs. Cool in the pan for about 15 minutes, then remove the cake from the pan, placing it onto a cooling rack.

On the stove, heat the apricot jelly to a pourable consistency. Use a pastry brush or spoon to brush the jelly over the cake (if desired).

Use a sieve to sprinkle the powdered sugar on the cake.

Tips

- Full-fat yogurt can easily work as a replacement for sour cream.
- The simplest way to remove the cake from the Bundt pan is to place a cooling rack on top of the pan, then flip it over and carefully lift the pan off. If you have any issues, use an offset spatula to loosen the cake from the side of the pan.
- Depending on your Bundt pan, you may want to butter and flour the pan instead of using cooking spray. Apply a thin layer of room-temperature butter around the inside of the pan using your hands or a pastry brush, then sprinkle in a couple of tablespoons of flour and shake it around the pan so that it coats the inside. Flip the Bundt pan over and tap out any excess flour before filling.

STRAWBERRY SCONES

I'm a sucker for a buttery, flaky scone. After a lot of trial and error, I discovered the secret to making strawberry scones that aren't soggy or too dry: dried strawberries. They not only distribute the strawberry flavor evenly throughout the scones but also make the scone buttery and flaky instead mushy. Now you have a seriously yummy scone and more time for coffee to make your morning better!

MAKES 8 SCONES

1 1/2 cups all-purpose flour

1 cup old-fashioned rolled oats

1/3 cup sugar

2 teaspoons baking powder

1/2 teaspoon salt

1/2 cup cold unsalted butter, cubed

2 cups freeze-dried strawberries

2 tablespoons cold sour cream

1/2 cup cold half-and-half

1 teaspoon vanilla extract

ICING

1 cup powdered sugar

1 tablespoon strawberry jelly or jam

1/2 to 1 tablespoon half-and-half

Combine the flour, oats, sugar, baking powder, and salt in a food processor and pulse to combine. Add the cold butter and pulse to combine until the butter breaks up and looks like small peas. Add the freeze-dried strawberries and pulse to combine.

In a separate small bowl, combine the sour cream, half-and-half, and vanilla extract. With the food processor running, add the liquid mixture into the flour mixture. Process until the mixture just starts to come together, being careful not to overmix.

Pour the mixture out onto a floured cutting board. Use your hand to press the dough together and into a round shape. Fold the dough in half and press it out again. Repeat once more, being careful not to overwork the dough. This folding process helps to create layers in the dough, which makes it lighter.

Press the dough into a round shape about 1 inch thick. Use a knife to cut the circle in half, then in half again to create a cross. Cut each quarter in half to create 8 slices. Place the slices onto a baking sheet and place in the freezer or fridge.

Preheat the oven to 375 degrees. Keep the scones in the fridge or freezer while the oven is heating up. Once the oven has heated, bake the scones for about 16 to 18 minutes or until the edges start to turn slightly golden.

While the scones cool, make the icing. In a medium bowl, whisk together the powdered sugar, jelly, and half-and-half. If the mixture is too thick, add more half-and-half a little at a time; if it is too thin, add more powdered sugar; do this until you achieve the consistency you like. When desired consistency is achieved, drizzle the icing over the cooled scones.

Tips

- If you wish to freeze the scones to bake at a later time, place the uncooked, cut scones in the freezer on the baking sheet. Once they are frozen, place them in a freezer-safe bag and label. Store in the freezer for up to three months.
- The scones can go straight from the freezer to the oven. Trust me, I have done this a million times. They may just need a few extra minutes to bake.
- Scones are best the day they are made.

Tips: Breakfast Boards

Every time I make a snackboard or a charcuterie board, it is devoured in seconds! Setting out all the food on one large board adds a communal feel, and that's my goal: to gather everyone together. So why not do this for breakfast too? You can get really intricate with these, or, if you are tight on time, you can put together some of your favorite store-bought items and elevate them with "from scratch" touches.

When I decide to make breakfast for my boys and my husband, certain—oh, how can I say this?—challenges arise. I guess I shouldn't be too surprised; I was a bit of a picky eater as a kid. When I'm preparing a family breakfast, the special orders come fast and furious. So when I discovered how to create my own breakfast boards, I was hooked! As they say, "Necessity is the mother of invention." Everyone gets a taste of their favorites, and they are a great way of introducing new food to that picky eater in your life. If you're lucky, you may be able to sneak a fruit and vegetable in there too. Here are two variations that are made to impress.

Breakfast Crostini Board

- Freshly toasted crusty bread
- Burrata
- Roasted tomatoes
- Pesto
- Scrambled eggs
- Fresh herbs
- Prosciutto

Pancake Breakfast Board

- Pancakes
- Bacon
- Fresh fruit
- Blueberry sauce
- Chocolate chips

Part Two

Celebrating Family

I owe everything to my family; they are my world. My parents are the reason I am so inspired by creativity. As huge supporters of the arts, they would take my sister and me to the theater or watch classic movies with us, and they made time to travel with us and take us to places like museums and exciting restaurants. My mom is a creative spirit. She sees beauty and potential in everything she lays her eyes on, especially when it comes to decorating. She always finds the extraordinary in the ordinary. One of the many things I love about my mom is how she included us in her crafts and baking. It was her firm belief that making things with your own two hands is the best way to show someone how much you care about them. She didn't realize how much she was inspiring me to one day share that same spirit of creativity and connection with my kids and with everyone I come in contact with.

Because of the environment my mom and dad created, I've always loved the arts—be it music, theater, or the art of a great meal. My parents believed in the arts so much that when I wanted to study theater in college as my major (with no backup plan), they were completely supportive. Their belief in me allowed me to feel like my dreams were, in fact, a future and not a wish. That love and support laid the foundation for my passion for family, food, and art.

My most cherished memories with my family are centered around the dinner table. We would spend hours at my grandpa Provenzano's house with all my aunts and uncles and cousins. This giant table was packed with pasta, meatballs, sauces, delicious breads, and everything else you can imagine. The whole place was packed with people, laughter, and tons of food; it was pure joy. I'd like to think we can bring some of that spirit into our everyday lives with our own families. Sure, the guest list may be a bit smaller, but the love and connection of family sharing a meal is the same.

"YOU'VE GOT THIS" POWER BREAKFAST

CREATIVE KID TIME

FAMILY PICNIC

FAVORITE FAMILY RECIPES

"YOU'VE GOT THIS" POWER BREAKFAST

When I was growing up, my mom would create surprise breakfasts for us that would wow the whole family. The best part: she didn't just do this for special events like a playoff game or opening night of a play. She would notice the *everyday moments*, like studying extra hard for a test, planning a school event, or practicing a speech. On what I thought was just another typical morning, I'd walk into the kitchen and on the table would be a breakfast especially for me! Seeing the effort my mom put in for me filled me with pride and confidence that she had my back. When you see someone in your house putting in the work, or if you're getting ready to tackle the new week, take a moment to feed your mind, body, and soul with a nourishing breakfast that will fill you up in more ways than one. And, if this meal is for someone special to you, seeing the look on their face when they realize that you went the extra mile to show up for them is something you both will treasure for years to come.

Set the Scene

Setting yourself and your family up for success is so important. Sure, a hearty meal to send your family off on their day is great, but little tokens of support and appreciation go a long way too. I love the idea of starting the day with a great breakfast. Fill your table with happiness and hearty food. Add decor that is themed for the big day, such as A+ napkins before a test. Pop a little gift on the table that they can take with them as a reminder of your support. A handwritten note on a napkin in a lunch bag, a picture slid into a notebook, or that extra-long hug before they head out the door will make your loved ones know that you have their backs and they can take on anything the world may throw at them.

Break a
leg today!
♡ Mom

"KNOT" JUST A GIFT: "BREAK A LEG" MACRAME KEY CHAIN

I truly believe good things come from hard work, and I'm also a believer in accentuating the positive—the old "good things in, good things out" mantra. Life throws challenges at all of us, and it's up to us how we face them. This "Break a Leg" DIY is perfect to remind you that you can tackle any obstacle head-on. The name is inspired by my years of doing theater and saying "Break a leg" before a show.

The art of knot-making is seen in a variety of cultures. Not only do I love how beautiful the knots are, but I also think there is something so uplifting about the symbolism of weaving the materials together to create a strong bond. (photo page 101)

MAKES 1 MACRAME KEY CHAIN

Macrame cord, cut into two
30-inch pieces

Scissors

Key ring

Fold one of the cords in half and place the folded part slightly through the key ring. Loop the ends around to go over the key ring and through the folded part (see photos on page 103). This is called a lark's head knot. Repeat with the other cord. You now have four cords to work with. The center two cords are the anchors and will not be moved, while the two outside cords will be the ones that you use.

Bring the right cord over and to the left of the two anchor cords to make a number 4 shape.

Place the left cord over the right cord.

Bring the left cord under the anchors and through the loop formed by the right cord and pull to create the knot.

Repeat the same steps, but starting with the left side.

Repeat, switching the starting side back and forth each time.

Continue until the desired length is achieved. Double knot to secure.

Tips

- The fringe at the bottom is optional but can be created by using a seam ripper or something similar to break up the ends of the cord.
- To create a twisted look, start on the same side each time, and the cord will twist as you go.
- If this is challenging, wrap threads of various colors around one piece of cord. Then tie the ends together about an inch from the bottom with more thread and secure with a dot of superglue.

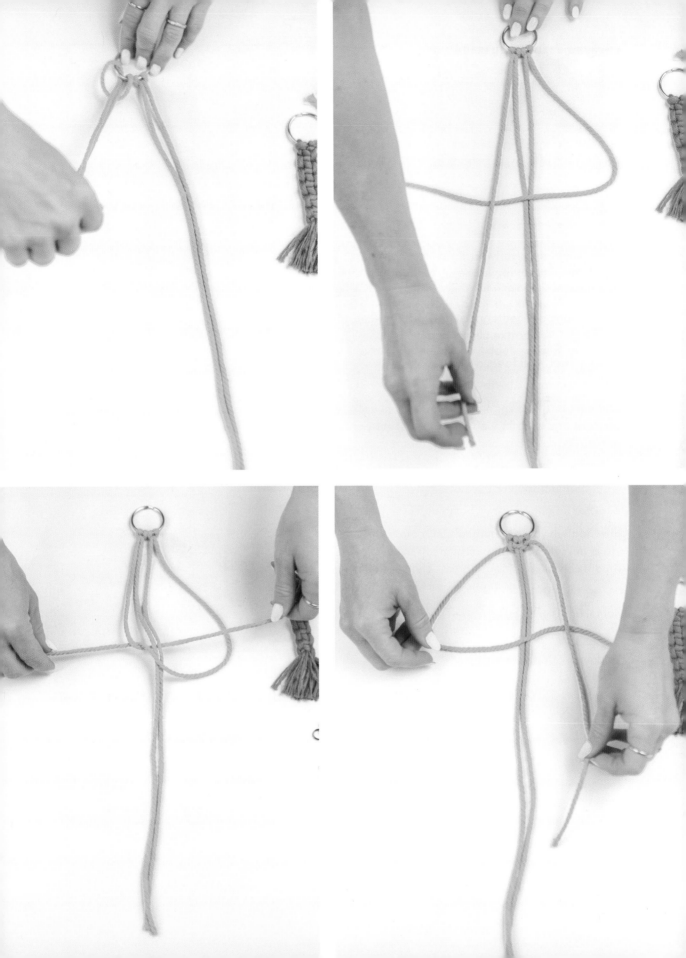

HEARTY BACON AND BREAKFAST POTATO HASH WITH CREAMY EGGS

Fact: this recipe will make you jump out of bed in the morning. My secret to good eggs: sour cream! That's right; this unexpected pairing works together to create fluffy, creamy eggs. I know it sounds a little out-there, but trust me on this one. This elevated version of a classic breakfast comes together quickly, so you won't have to wait long if you rise and shine with an empty stomach.

MAKES 4 SERVINGS

BREAKFAST POTATOES

1 pound potatoes, cut into about 1-inch pieces (cubes or slices)

1 tablespoon plus 1 teaspoon salt, divided

6 to 8 slices of thick bacon

3 tablespoons olive oil or sunflower seed oil

1 large or 2 small red bell peppers, cut into small pieces

1/2 onion, diced

1 jalapeño pepper, rims and seeds removed for less spice or retained for extra spice, cut into very small pieces

1/4 to 1/2 teaspoon cumin

1/2 teaspoon chili powder

1 tablespoon unsalted butter

CREAMY EGGS

2 tablespoons unsalted butter

4 to 5 large eggs

1/8 cup full-fat sour cream, room temperature

TOPPINGS

Cilantro or parsley, chopped

Place the potatoes into a large pot and fill with cold water so the potatoes are covered by a couple of inches of water. Add a tablespoon of salt. Bring the water to a boil, then reduce to a gentle boil until the potatoes are tender; drain.

Place the bacon in a large skillet over medium heat and cook until crispy, flipping as needed. Place the bacon on a paper towel after cooking to remove excess oil.

Heat the olive oil or sunflower seed oil in another large skillet over medium heat. Cook the bell peppers, onions, jalapeños, and 1/2 teaspoon of salt until softened. Add the potatoes and cook on high until the potatoes start to brown; it helps to use a spatula to press them into the pan, even if they get smashed a bit, and leave the mixture alone to brown, then flip it over.

Once the potatoes are browning, add in the cumin, chili powder, and butter, and allow the potatoes to cook and brown a bit more. Add the additional 1/2 teaspoon of salt if needed.

For the creamy eggs: In a small skillet over low heat, melt the butter, then add the eggs. Use a rubber spatula to continuously stir the eggs around, breaking the yolks, until the eggs start to cook and come together. When the eggs are close to being done, stir in the sour cream. Remove the eggs from the heat before they are completely cooked, since they will continue to cook.

Place the potatoes on a plate and top with the creamy eggs; crumble the bacon over the top and sprinkle with freshly cut herbs. Serve hot.

CHAMPIONS BROWN SUGAR SOUR CREAM PANCAKES

Buttermilk gets all the love when it comes to pancakes, but have you tried sour cream? Its richness and acidity create a light and fluffy treat. I add brown sugar for a depth of flavor and a touch of sweetness. These pancakes are a celebration in themselves.

MAKES 15 TO 18 PANCAKES

1 cup milk

1/2 cup sour cream

2 large eggs

5 tablespoons unsalted butter, divided: 2 tablespoons melted and cooled slightly, 3 tablespoons reserved for greasing the pan

1 teaspoon vanilla extract

1 1/2 cups all-purpose flour

1/4 cup firmly packed brown sugar

1 teaspoon baking powder

1 teaspoon baking soda

1/2 teaspoon salt

Maple syrup for serving

In a large bowl, whisk together the milk, sour cream, eggs, melted butter, and vanilla extract.

In a separate large bowl, whisk together the flour, brown sugar, baking powder, baking soda, and salt.

Stir the wet mixture into the dry mixture until just combined. The batter will be lumpy.

Melt about 1/2 tablespoon of butter in a large nonstick skillet, or pancake griddle, over medium-low heat until the butter is lightly bubbling and light brown.

Ladle about 1/4 cup of the batter for one pancake. Cook 3 to 4 minutes, until bubbles form on top of each pancake and the bottoms start to become golden brown.

Flip the pancakes. Cook 1 to 2 minutes, until the other side is golden brown.

Carefully wipe out any excess browned butter with paper towels. Repeat with the remaining butter and pancake batter. Serve warm with warm maple syrup.

Tips

- I recommend using room temperature ingredients to allow everything to mix well.
- Save yourself time and sanity by making and freezing these ahead of time. Simply place the cooled pancakes into a freezer-safe container. I like to separate them by placing either wax paper or parchment paper between each pancake so they do not stick together.
- Pancakes can be a labor of love, and the person making the pancakes sometimes is the last to eat them. If you make the pancakes in batches, place the cooked ones in a heated oven at about 175 to 200 degrees to keep them warm while you finish cooking.

BREAKFAST BANANA SPLIT WITH HOMEMADE GRANOLA

Instead of topping a banana with ice cream and crunchy toppings, I love to use creamy yogurt, crunchy homemade granola, and fresh fruit for a healthy power breakfast. This dessert-for-breakfast combo is so good it will turn you into a morning person. (photo page 98)

MAKES 1 SERVING

1 banana

½ cup yogurt (I like using Greek yogurt)

Homemade Granola (add as much as you like)

Berries (any kind—add as much as you like)

Cut the banana down the middle so that it's "split" and place it into a bowl or container. Top it with the yogurt, granola, and berries.

HOMEMADE GRANOLA

MAKES 9 TO 10 CUPS

8 tablespoons unrefined coconut oil or unsalted butter

½ cup honey

2 teaspoons vanilla extract

4 cups old-fashioned rolled oats

½ cup unsweetened shredded coconut (if you can't find unsweetened, you can use sweetened)

¼ cup wheat germ, optional

1 cup sunflower seeds

1 cup pepita seeds (aka shelled pumpkin seeds)

1 tablespoon sesame seeds

½ teaspoon salt (I like using kosher)

1 teaspoon cinnamon

½ teaspoon nutmeg

¼ teaspoon allspice

Preheat the oven to 325 degrees.

In a pan over medium heat, melt the coconut oil or butter with the honey. When the oil has melted, add the vanilla extract.

In a large bowl, add the rolled oats, shredded coconut, wheat germ (if using), sunflower seeds, pepita seeds, sesame seeds, salt, cinnamon, nutmeg, and allspice, and toss to combine.

Pour the honey mixture over the dry ingredients and stir together using a rubber spatula.

Line two baking sheets with parchment paper and evenly spread the oat mixture between the two. Press together with the spatula so that the oats stick together; this creates the large "chunks" when you break the granola apart after baking. Bake for 12 to 14 minutes, until the edges start to brown slightly. For extra crunchy granola, bake for an additional 3 to 5 minutes, making sure it doesn't brown too much.

Remove the granola from the oven and allow it to cool completely. Use your hands to break up the large piece and serve. Store in an airtight container for 2 weeks.

Tips

- Take this to go by deconstructing it and turning it into a parfait by layering it in a mason jar.
- I love having granola around! My mom would keep it in a clear container with a lid so that we could snack on it, and I do the same at my house.
- Make sure the granola is completely cool before you break it up. That way you get big chunks of granola instead of crumbs.
- My favorite fruits to use on top are strawberries, raspberries, and blueberries. If you want to make it extra fun, add a sprinkle of chocolate chips.

Tips: Make It To Go

There are some mornings when you have to hustle out before the sun rises. After the number of mornings I spent quietly leaving my house to get to set at five thirty, go to hair and makeup, prep my segments, and basically have an entire day before nine o'clock, I became an expert in packing on-the-go breakfasts. My favorite comes in the form of a jar. I *love* to create a pretty little parfait in a mason jar with layers of yogurt, fruit, and Homemade Granola (page 107). Overnight oats is an easy make-ahead breakfast that barely takes any time to prepare. It's another way to make use of those mason jars. If you have an extra moment in the morning, brûlée up a few bananas for some extra flavor!

BRÛLÉED BANANA OVERNIGHT OATS

MAKES 1 SERVING

½ cup oats (regular or old-fashioned)

½ cup hemp milk (or milk of choice)

1 tablespoon chia seeds

¼ teaspoon cinnamon

1 banana

1 to 2 tablespoons sugar (regular or coconut sugar)

1 to 2 tablespoons honey, optional for topping

Pour the oats, milk, chia seeds, and cinnamon in a jar and mix with a spoon. Cover with a lid and allow to sit overnight.

In the morning, line a baking sheet with aluminum foil and turn on the broiler.

Cut the banana into slices on an angle. Place the cut banana slices on the baking sheet and sprinkle with sugar.

Place the baking sheet under the broiler, and make sure the rack is close to the broiler so the sugar on the bananas will become lightly golden. Watch the bananas carefully as they start to caramelize. It will happen quickly, and you do not want them to burn.

Once the bananas are brûléed (the sugar has begun to brown), remove the baking sheet from the oven and allow the bananas to cool until they are able to be touched.

Give the oats a quick stir, then top them with the bananas and a drizzle of honey.

CREATIVE KID TIME

Let's get creative! I always love to see when my little guys use their imagination to express themselves in ways I could never predict. I think it's so important to encourage our kids to use their creativity. When they do, their confidence in what they can accomplish will grow. I'm such an advocate for creativity because it allows us to dig deep into our minds to express ourselves and share more of ourselves with the world. In that spirit, get with your kids and see what kind of snacks you can dream up together. I know you'll be surprised and delighted with the results when your creativity starts flowing!

Set the Scene

Creative kid time starts with supplies. I like to have some crafts that are shared and some that are personal. Sharing can prove to be a tough thing for some kids, and it should be encouraged, but there is also something powerful about a child having their own supplies and taking responsibility for them. I like giving each child an "art toolbox" of their own. This could be an actual toolbox or a cart or bin with supplies—anything that they can take ownership of. Fill it with supplies, and guide them on how to care for their creative goodies.

POPSICLE STICK JAR OF CREATIVITY

"Mom, I'm bored!" is one of my least favorite phrases. I know it drives every parent crazy. Creativity is always a good answer, but sometimes you can run out of ideas. A fun way to get the ball rolling is to draw ideas from a hat—or in this case, popsicle sticks from a jar! (photo page 113)

MAKES 1 JAR

Painter's tape

Popsicle sticks, one per idea

Acrylic craft paint in three different colors

Paintbrush

Marker with a fine tip (preferably a Sharpie)

Mason jar or large jar

Use the painter's tape to mark off the top part of each popsicle stick about an inch or two from the end. Paint one side of the sticks. Use one color for indoor ideas, one for outdoor ideas, and one for out-of-the-house adventures.

Once dry, paint the other side as well (optional).

Once the sticks are dry, use a marker to write your ideas. Store the popsicle sticks in a jar.

Tips

- Let the kids take the lead. Have them come up with the ideas, shop for supplies, and paint and write on the sticks.
- Create a label to cover the jar so that you can't see what you are picking.
- Photograph the activity you choose and save it in a book or box. When the jar is empty, you can look back at all you accomplished!

List Ideas

- Make a book.
- Camp in the backyard.
- Come up with your own recipe.
- Create and act out your own play.
- Write and mail five letters to family and friends.
- Create a vision board.
- Go for a hike.
- Learn to make a paper airplane.
- Paint a picture.
- Plant a tree.
- Bake a pie.
- Go to the library.
- Play a board game.
- Make popcorn and watch a movie.
- Paint rocks.
- Go to a museum.
- Make puppets and put on a show.
- Make your own journal to write in.
- Draw a chalk picture on the sidewalk.

KID-FRIENDLY VEGGIE CREATIONS AND FRUIT TOWERS

So many life lessons are taught in the kitchen. There, kids can develop appreciation for the work that goes into making the food, including learning where the food came from, why food quality is so important, how to troubleshoot when something goes wrong, and how to multitask. They'll also practice counting, measuring, patience, teamwork—the list goes on and on! I find that kids tend to eat a wider variety of foods, including fruits and veggies, when they help put meals together—especially if they can be creative while cooking. Take a simple rice cake; on its own it's kind of bland, but adding a few fruits and veggies makes it a more vibrant and delicious snack. (photo page 116)

MAKES AS MANY CREATIONS AS YOU CAN IMAGINE

Variety of veggies

Variety of fruit

Kids' knives

Cutting boards

Dips and spreads, such as peanut butter, sunflower seed butter, yogurt, cream cheese, etc.

Additional snack food (pretzels, Goldfish crackers, animal crackers, cheese, lunch meat, etc.)

Candy eyes

Popsicle sticks

Toothpicks and/or kabob skewers

Food-grade butcher paper, optional

Offset spatulas, optional (but great for spreading)

Choose a theme, such as animals, bugs, or a train.

After teaching the kids how to cut properly, allow them to cut the easily prepared fruits and veggies on their own cutting boards while you prepare those that require more skill.

Spread out the fruit and veggies along with the dips and additional snack food, and turn the kids loose to make their own creations on the theme you've chosen.

Give them examples of how they can use the popsicle sticks, toothpicks/skewers, spatulas, and edible ingredients to assemble their snacks.

Grab a platter and display the creations before serving or saving for later.

Tips for Teaching Kids to Use Knives

- Start with kids' knives. It's the safest way to get them used to the feel of cutting.
- Show them proper cutting techniques. The most important technique to teach them, in my opinion, is to make a claw with their non-cutting hand to keep their fingers away from the blade.
- Start with small stuff, such as strawberries, bananas, and anything soft.
- Include the kids in dinner prep so they can see how their work helps create something bigger.

THE SNACKBOARD SOLUTION

When my kids come home from school—or basically at any given point in the day—they are "starving." They are bottomless pits! My solution: a snackboard. It's like a kid's version of a charcuterie board. I fill a cutting board with all the snacks they love, plus food I'm trying to get them to eat more of, like veggies. I find that my kids and their friends eat a surprising amount of veggies when they're included in a board that looks appealing and fun. It's all about the variety!

Something salty and crunchy: Include at least two kinds of crackers or pretzels. This is also a good time to add a gluten-free option without the kids knowing.

Something sweet: I don't add "treats" because I want this board to be focused on the "snacking" aspect. Instead, I provide fresh or dried fruit. This is also a great way to present fruit they haven't tried yet to get them tasting new things.

Veggies always: Veggies always seem to taste better when they are cut and displayed in a cute way. Go for crunchy carrots, cucumber, peppers, and celery.

Cheese: On adult boards, it's completely fine to have little knives for cutting, but that's not the best idea for kids. Instead, provide cheese slices or cubes.

Dips: On big boards, I like having two separate dips, even if it's just the same dip in two different bowls. It prevents arguments over who was dipping first (cue eye roll). Ranch and hummus are the top two favorites in our house.

Get creative: Snackboards have a huge "wow" factor for kids. Every time I put one together, they get so excited, and when it's done, they are always impressed. These are easy to customize for holidays and seasons. Make one that is all green for St. Patrick's Day or all pink and red for Valentine's Day, or create a letter with all the food for someone's birthday. The options are endless.

ICE CREAM IN A BAG WITH HOMEMADE SPRINKLES

Did you know that you can make ice cream in a bag? No joke! And it's the perfect way to teach kids a quick lesson about science. This is fun all year round, but it's an exciting project to do on a hot summer day. I also like to top mine with some homemade sprinkles.

MAKES 1 SERVING

1 cup half-and-half or cream

1 cup whole milk

1/4 cup extra-fine sugar or maple syrup

1/4 teaspoon vanilla extract

4 sealable plastic bags (2 sandwich- or quart-size, 2 gallon-size)

1 cup kosher salt or ice cream salt

Plastic container, optional

Add the half-and-half, milk, sugar, and vanilla extract into a small plastic bag. Remove the air, seal tightly, and double bag the liquid to prevent salt from getting into the bag.

Fill the large plastic bag a little over halfway with ice, and add about a cup of salt.

Place the small bag into the larger bag and seal. Place this into the second gallon-size plastic bag and seal. Shake for about 10 minutes.

Remove the ice cream from the bags and serve or store in the freezer.

Tips

- Double bag the ice cream ingredients *and* double bag the ice. It can get messy if you don't.
- Yes, it takes 10 minutes—but that's what makes it fun!
- Cover the bags with a towel if your hands get too cold during the shaking process.

HOMEMADE SPRINKLES

MAKES ABOUT 4 CUPS
OF SPRINKLES

4 cups powdered sugar, sifted

1/4 cup meringue powder

1 tablespoon freshly squeezed
lemon juice

1 teaspoon vanilla extract

4 to 6 tablespoons water

Gel food coloring

Mix the powdered sugar and meringue powder together in a stand mixer with a whisk attachment.

With the mixer on low, stir in the lemon juice, vanilla extract, and 4 tablespoons of water. Once mixed, increase the speed to medium-high and beat until thick, about 15 minutes. If the mixture is too thick, add the additional 1 to 2 tablespoons of water until the mixture is able to be piped through a piping bag with a small tip.

Divide the mixture into separate bowls and add the food colorings of your choice; mix until well combined. Scoop the colored mixtures into piping bags with a small round tip.

Cover a baking sheet with a silicone mat, parchment paper, or wax paper, and pipe a long, thin line of the sprinkle "batter." Repeat with each of the colors. Let the icing strips dry for about 24 hours.

You can use a knife or simply break up the strips with your hands to create the sprinkles.

Tips: Empower Your Kids

These tips can help your kids build confidence in the kitchen and creativity in life:

- Allow them to make their own decisions about how they want to prepare their food.
- Include them in the grocery shopping.
- Give them space in the kitchen to make mistakes.
- Make a mess! Letting the kitchen be a space where it isn't taboo to spill allows the kids to know that they are free to create.
- They also need to clean up. I encourage making messes, but cleaning up after is an important part of knowing the work that goes into preparing food.

FAMILY PICNIC

When I was growing up, my mom would send my sister and me outside to play no matter what. Rain, shine, snow—you name it, we were out in it. At the time, I would grumble and pout, but I realized that logging time in Mother Nature taught me to relish the great outdoors, explore my community, and use my imagination. While my mother's intention may have been to tire us out, being outside taught us to be grateful for the epic beauty of nature.

That's why this section is all about celebrating picnic-style! Having a picnic is the perfect way to spend time together as a family, bask in nature, and—even if you're in your backyard—create those magical little moments that make you feel like you're on a mini adventure. So grab a blanket, slap on some sunscreen, and head outside for some good conversation and even better company.

Set the Scene

There's no better way to soak in the outdoors than with a picnic, but creating that picturesque scene takes a little bit of thoughtful prep. Throwing the perfect picnic requires a few factors like the location, the proper placement of a waterproof blanket, and the ease of serving. Lastly, prechill your bubbly or cooler drinks before you pack up for the best portable feast. Bring a big enough blanket for everyone in your party to sit on. DIY personalized tables not only make sitting more comfortable but also are fun to make. Elevate your layout with a small bouquet of flowers to add ambiance. I like to place mine in jars and then set those jars into baskets for a classic picnic look. Remember that the food needs to be portable. Jars are great for drinks and salads, and I love packing sandwiches in parchment paper for a vintage touch.

PERSONALIZED TABLES

These DIY trays instantly take your picnic spread to the next level. I will let you in on a little secret, though; while these trays may look elevated, they are just store-bought breakfast-in-bed trays (with a personalized touch, of course). Monogram your tray or get artsy with it. Indulge your artistic side and create a piece that is sure to be a conversation starter. These trays can also be given as souvenirs from your time together. (photo pages 124 and 127)

MAKES 1 TABLE

Breakfast-in-bed tray with legs

Nontoxic acrylic paint

Paintbrush

Monogram lettering made with vinyl using a cutting machine or cut from paper

A nontoxic water-based sealer (e.g., Mod Podge's dishwasher-safe water-based sealer)

Paint the trays as desired with the acrylic craft paint. Let your kids paint their own to make it extra fun! Let dry.

If using vinyl letters, simply attach according to the vinyl brand's directions.

If using paper, apply a thin layer of the water-based sealer onto the desired area of the board and place the letter onto the adhesive. Allow it to dry completely and then seal the entire area with more water-based sealer.

Tips

- Keep in mind that these trays are meant to be used as tables, not to replace dishes. I do not recommend eating directly off the trays or cutting on the trays if paint or adhesive has been applied.
- If you use a sealer, make sure to seal the entire area; this can add a glossy finish. If you seal only one area, the finish will not be cohesive. Be sure to cover evenly.
- If you do not want to change too much of the trays by painting them, you can simply add a pretty monogram on the side or another part of the tray.
- I recommend getting trays that have legs on them versus flat trays. That will give you a look and feel of an individual table.
- For easy transport, look for trays that are either stackable or have legs that can fold.

THREE-BEAN SALAD IN A JAR

Mason jars are not only easy on the eyes but also make packing for a picnic super easy. This recipe is my attempt to re-create the three-bean salad that I used to order at a posh LA hotspot when I was running around from audition to audition when I first moved to Hollywood. I hope it will help you channel your inner A-lister. (photo page 124)

MAKES 4 SERVINGS

1 (15-ounce) can chickpeas, drained and rinsed

1 (15-ounce) can black beans, drained and rinsed

1 (15-ounce) can kidney beans, drained and rinsed

1 cup diced red bell pepper

1 English cucumber, halved lengthwise and diced

1 pint cherry tomatoes, halved or quartered, depending on size

1/2 cup diced red onion

1 teaspoon freshly chopped oregano

1/4 cup freshly chopped flat-leaf parsley

3/4 cup brined artichokes, chopped, then measured

Kosher salt and freshly ground black pepper to taste

SALAD DRESSING

1/4 cup extra-virgin olive oil

1 tablespoon freshly squeezed lemon juice

2 tablespoons red wine vinegar

1 tablespoon honey

1 garlic clove, minced

1 teaspoon Dijon mustard

1 teaspoon fresh oregano, roughly chopped

Kosher salt and pepper to taste

In a large bowl, add the chickpeas, black beans, kidney beans, bell pepper, cucumber, cherry tomatoes, red onions, oregano, parsley, artichokes, and salt and pepper, and use a spoon to combine.

Make the dressing: Place the olive oil, lemon juice, red wine vinegar, honey, garlic, Dijon mustard, oregano, and salt and pepper in a bowl and whisk to combine. You can also add all of these to a mason jar with a lid and shake everything together.

Pour the dressing over the salad and toss to combine. Add additional salt, pepper, or lemon juice if needed.

Allow the mixture to sit in the fridge for about 30 minutes before serving. Pack in mason jars to take to your picnic.

BLAT (BACON, LETTUCE, AVOCADO, AND TOMATO) SANDWICH

Sandwiches belong in the picnic food hall of fame. And the MVP is the BLT! I love the classic BLT, but avocado takes this sandwich from benchwarmer to all-star. My secret ingredient for the perfect BLAT sandwich is Herby Ranch instead of mayo. It adds an extra herbaceous, tangy flavor. I like to wrap my sandwiches in parchment paper; it was something my mom always did when we were growing up, so it makes me feel like she's on every picnic with me.

Make this sandwich picnic-friendly by using sturdy bread. I like using a fresh baguette because it will soak in that great ranch flavor while staying crispy on the outside.

MAKES 1 12-INCH SANDWICH

1 (12-inch) baguette

1/2 avocado, skin and pit removed, cut into slices

Freshly squeezed lemon juice to taste

Salt and pepper to taste

3 to 4 slices cooked bacon

1 tomato, cut into slices

1/2 to 1 cup arugula

2 tablespoons Herby Ranch (page 14)

Cut the baguette down the center to create a top and bottom.

Layer the bottom with the sliced avocado and add a squeeze of fresh lemon juice and a light sprinkle of salt and pepper over the avocado. Top the avocado with the bacon slices, tomato, and arugula.

Drizzle the Herby Ranch over the ingredients and place the top onto the sandwich.

Wrap the sandwich tightly in parchment paper and tie with string. Use a serrated knife to cut the sandwich or wait to cut it at the picnic.

Tips

- Using freshly cooked bacon makes a huge difference! It's crunchier and saltier than if you make it ahead of time and store it in the fridge.
- The lemon juice on the avocado prevents it from getting brown and also adds a nice tanginess that balances out the flavors.
- Add crushed red pepper flakes for an element of heat.
- Bring extra ranch in a jar in case you want to dip!

BLACKBERRY ITALIAN SODAS

Did you know "Italian" sodas were actually created in the United States? I will say, Italian Americans adore them. These sodas are a refreshing way to get that bubbly flavored drink taste by using fresh fruit syrup. If you want to make this extra special for your picnic, you can can turn the sodas into desserts by adding in a scoop of ice cream—*boom*, you have yourself a float.

MAKES 1 SERVING

Ice

1/4 cup Blackberry Fruit Syrup (page 133); add more or less to taste

1 cup carbonated water

1/2 cup ice cream, optional

Fill a large cup with ice. Pour the fruit syrup over the ice. Pour the carbonated water over the syrup and give it a gentle mix with a spoon.

Optional: replace the ice with 1/2 cup ice cream.

BLACKBERRY FRUIT SYRUP

MAKES 1 SERVING

1 cup sugar

1 cup water

1 pound blackberries

1 tablespoon lemon juice

Add the sugar and water to a medium saucepan and bring to a boil. Cook until the sugar has dissolved, stirring frequently.

Stir in the berries and cook for another 10 minutes, stirring frequently and using a wooden spoon to gently press the berries to release their juice.

Using a fine mesh sieve, strain the mixture into a small bowl. Stir in the lemon juice.

Let the mixture cool before adding it into the drinks.

Tips

- Add a slight creaminess without the extra sugar by including a splash of half-and-half instead of the ice cream.
- You can use other berries, such as blueberries, raspberries, or strawberries, instead of blackberries.
- Don't overmix! You don't want to lose the bubbles.
- If you plan to make these at your family picnic, make sure all the items stay cold on the road by adding ice packs to your cooler.

FRUIT AND BROWNIE KABOBS

These adorable little skewers can be customized in just about any way you like. Get the kids involved with the prep for even more family-friendly fun. We love brownies, and fruit complements chocolate, so fruit and brownie kabobs are our go-to.

MAKES AS MANY KABOBS
AS YOU HAVE FRUIT AND
BROWNIES TO SKEWER

Fruit options:
Strawberries
Blueberries
Grapes
Blackberries
Cherries
Brownies (page 135), cut
into 1-inch cubes
Kabob skewers

Cut the fruit if needed. For example, blueberries do not need to be cut but large strawberries may need to be cut in half.

Alternate adding the brownie pieces and the fruit onto the kabobs as desired. Allow the picnic-goers to make their own for an added touch of fun.

BROWNIES

MAKES ONE 9 X 13-INCH PAN

1 cup plus 2 tablespoons
unsalted butter, divided
1 1/2 cups all-purpose or white
whole wheat flour; reserve
1/4 cup for flouring
4 ounces unsweetened chocolate
1 teaspoon baking powder
1 teaspoon salt
2 cups sugar
4 large eggs, room temperature
1 teaspoon vanilla extract

Preheat the oven to 350 degrees.

Butter and flour a 9 x 13-inch baking pan by wiping the inside of the pan with the two additional tablespoons of butter, then sprinkling in enough of the reserved flour to coat the butter. Flip the pan over the sink and lightly tap it to remove excess flour.

Place the remaining butter and chocolate into a large, heatproof bowl over a pan of simmering water, making sure the water isn't high enough to touch the bowl. You can also melt the chocolate and butter in the microwave, but be careful not to overcook or burn it. Once the butter and chocolate are melted together, set the bowl aside to cool.

In a bowl, whisk the flour, baking powder, and salt. Set aside.

Once the butter and chocolate have cooled, whisk in the sugar. Then whisk in the eggs one at a time, making sure each one is well incorporated. Whisk in the vanilla extract.

Pour the flour into the chocolate mixture in small increments, whisking each time. Mix until just combined.

Pour the brownie batter into the prepared baking pan; use a spatula to make sure it is spread evenly around the pan.

Bake at 350 degrees for 25 to 30 minutes or until a toothpick comes out mostly clean; it is okay to underbake these slightly. You can tell they are done if the middle is set.

Allow the brownies to cool completely before cutting into approximately 1-inch cubes.

Tips

- This can be a project for kids to prepare at home or while enjoying the picnic. Either way, the enjoyment is really in the making of the kabobs as well as the eating.
- Some kabobs can be all fruit, fruit and brownie combinations, or just brownies.
- Use cookie cutters to create shapes or even cut out letters to spell a name.

Tips: Make the Most of the Seasons

Host a get-together that stands out from the rest by highlighting the season! Small details that showcase the current time of year are what make for a memorable celebration. Here are some of my favorite tips that will help you enjoy every moment of the season you are in.

Fall: Collecting leaves is a great pastime for any fall picnic. Searching out leaves and curating the most special ones is a great way to connect with other picnic-goers. It's an especially thoughtful way to bond with the kids who may be in attendance. Bring a book or two to the picnic so you can place the leaves between the pages to flatten them. Not only will this preserve the leaves, but it also makes a sweet keepsake for the occasion. Another option for your fall picnics is pumpkin decorating. This is a perfect fall-themed craft that is great to do outside, whether you're full-out carving or simply painting or gluing on craft supplies.

Winter: Do you want to build a snowman? Because I certainly do! Have a snowman-building contest with the kiddos. Award prizes for the fastest assembled, the most creative, the tallest, and so on. You might be saying to yourself, *A winter picnic, no thank you, Maria,* but there is nothing like warm food and piping hot drinks on a cold day. Bring your food in an insulated food bag and drinks in thermoses. Sitting in the snow makes the chilly winter dining experience unexpectedly fun.

Spring: When spring is in the air, the birds are singing, and the flowers are opening up, it's hard to keep anyone indoors! Spring weather can be hit or miss, so keep that in mind when planning your spring events. Bring out the games that don't require sitting in case the ground is slightly damp from the spring showers. Classic games like croquet, ring toss, lawn bowling, and bean bag toss (to name a few) are perfect for having some laughs and getting everyone to participate.

Summer: If the sun's out, I'm out too! When summer is in full swing, outdoor events are a must. Activities like scavenger hunts are great in the summer because everything is in bloom, and they get all of your guests active and moving. Create a list of flowers, bugs, plants, rocks, and so on. Each person can fill a basket with these items, and the first person to find them all wins. Stay cool by packing things like frozen fruit, frozen yogurt, and frozen lemonade.

FAVORITE
FAMILY
RECIPES

Every family has their own special recipes. Family recipes hold so many memories, and every time you taste or smell a particular dish, you are transported back to another time. I think that's why I love food so much: it is connected to moments of togetherness. This is also why I believe meeting for a meal is a great way to create new memories with your crew. It doesn't matter if you are getting together with coworkers, roommates, neighbors, friends, or whatever your family unit is. When you create recipes together, you create memories that will last a lifetime.

Set the Scene

When I was growing up, I looked forward to family dinners. Everyone gathered together, all my favorite dishes lining the table—I was in heaven! I think it's important that our kids know they can count on having dinner as a family. Though they might not realize it now, these family dinners are something they will look back on as special. Thinking back to those times, I now know I was learning life lessons at our family dinners, even though I was only focused on the spaghetti. When I would come home from school, I knew that my house would smell like whatever was for dinner that night. Whenever I saw my mom bringing out the special emerald china, I knew we were in store for a fancy dinner. Grandpa Provenzano would always have a red-and-white checked tablecloth on his table when we would have pasta.

These small yet consistent acts are the epitome of everyday celebrations. Moments like these all by themselves may not seem significant, but strung together for many years, they build the traditions that make a house a home and showcase the importance of family. Every time I make a family recipe and share it with my kids, my heart feels full. I feel like I am carrying on a legacy of togetherness, and it's all centered around the dinner table. Create your own memories in your home with unique traditions.

LAZY SUSAN GAME BOARD

One of my favorite ways to hang out as a family is with a good old-fashioned board game. In this day and age, it's such a treat to be able to have fun without having to plug something in or look at a screen. Watching my kids strategize and be surprised on board game night is more fun than even playing the game!

When playing board games, we often find ourselves having to reach over to move pieces or spin the spinner. I thought using a lazy Susan would make game night a bit easier. I love the idea of customizing the board so that it's unique to you and your crew. When you are playing a game that doesn't require the board, you can load it up with snacks and spin the board to pass the snacks around the table. (photo page 141)

MAKES 1 LAZY SUSAN

2 wood rounds (around 14 inches in diameter and 1 inch thick)

Paint, wood stain, and/or vinyl for decorating

Lazy Susan hardware

Industrial-strength glue

Decorate the wood rounds as desired with paint, wood stain, vinyl, etc.

Once decorated, flip one of the wood rounds over to attach the lazy Susan hardware with the industrial-strength glue. Allow it to dry completely. Apply the industrial-strength glue to the center of the second wood round. Press the lazy Susan hardware (with the first round on top) into the glue on the second round so that the hardware is sandwiched between the two rounds. Allow it to cure overnight.

Tips

- Customize it! Use a cutting machine to add details like your family name, cute sayings, themed colors, and so on.
- Decorate both wood rounds so that each "top" of the lazy Susan can be used.
- When using the lazy Susan for food, serve the food on a plate or another food-safe item.
- To preserve your design on each side, place the finished lazy Susan on a piece of felt or another piece of fabric to prevent any scratches from use.
- Yes, the glue will work! I like using a Gorilla Glue that is a gel texture and waterproof. Make sure the glue you choose works well on wood and metal.

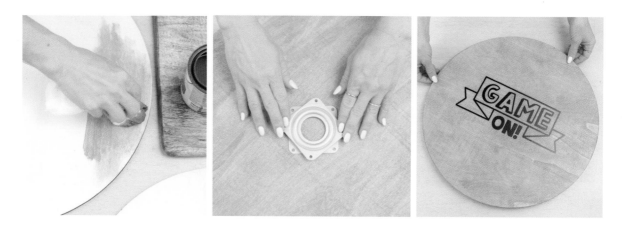

MARINARA WITH ANGEL-HAIR PASTA AND PESTO

Every holiday season when I was growing up, we would visit my aunt Rose, who lived in Chicago. We would dress up, go to the theater, see a show, and then go to dinner. One of our favorite restaurants was an Italian one (shocking), and they made angel-hair pasta topped with marinara and pesto. I remember all of us being so enamored with the pasta that my mom went home and re-created it, much to our delight. Now I create this recipe and love adding my Lemony Basil Pesto (page 51). (photo pages 144–45)

MAKES 4 SERVINGS

Salt to taste

1 pound dried angel-hair pasta

4 cups Homemade Marinara Sauce (page 143)

4 to 8 tablespoons Lemony Basil Pesto for topping (page 51)

Bring a large pot of water to a boil and add enough salt to flavor the water. Cook the pasta until al dente.

Drain the pasta and put it back in the pot. Add 2 to 3 cups of marinara, and cook the pasta in the marinara over low heat for a couple of minutes.

Scoop the pasta into bowls and top with extra sauce and a scoop of pesto (about 1 to 2 tablespoons).

HOMEMADE MARINARA SAUCE

MAKES ABOUT 13 CUPS OF SAUCE

3 tablespoons olive oil

1/8 cup minced garlic (about 8 cloves)

1 cup red or white wine

3 (28-ounce) cans crushed tomatoes

1 (28-ounce) can diced tomatoes

1 tablespoon dried oregano

1 tablespoon dried basil

2 teaspoons dried thyme

1 teaspoon dried rosemary

Salt and pepper to taste

Warm the olive oil in a large pot over medium heat. Lightly sauté the garlic in the olive oil, being careful not to let the garlic brown. Add the wine and cook for one minute.

Stir in the crushed tomatoes and diced tomatoes. Stir in the oregano, basil, thyme, and rosemary.

Bring the sauce to a boil, then reduce the heat to low. Simmer on low for an hour or two, stirring regularly.

Remove from heat and puree the sauce with an immersion blender, or transfer to a standard blender to blend. If you like a chunkier sauce, you can omit this step.

Simmer the sauce for another half hour. Adjust the seasonings at this point, adding salt, pepper, or more herbs as needed.

Tips

- I like to use San Marzano tomatoes for both the crushed and diced tomatoes.
- Red wine will add a deep, rich flavor, while white wine will bring out a bright and acidic taste.
- If I'm using dried herbs, I like to rub them in my hands as I pour them into the sauce to release the flavor.
- Before serving, I like to add fresh herbs into the sauce—whatever I have on hand, such as basil or parsley. Simply sprinkle the herbs over the finished dish.

MOM'S GERMAN PANCAKES

Just the smell of these crispy yet chewy pancakes right out of the frying pan instantly transports me back to my childhood. My mom had the hardest time giving me exact measurements for this recipe. It reminds me a bit of making pasta, because the texture for the batter is really something you have to get a feel for as you make it. This recipe has such basic ingredients, but when you fry these little pancakes up, you will know why we love them so much. These are not meant to be served with syrup, though. Nope! Fold them in half and then dip them in jelly.

MAKES 4 SERVINGS

1 1/4 cups flour, plus more if needed

1/4 teaspoon of salt

1 large egg, room temperature

1 cup whole milk, room temperature, plus more if needed

2 cups shortening

Combine flour and salt in a large bowl. Whisk in the egg and milk.

Place a large frying pan on medium heat and add enough shortening so that it fills about 1/2 inch of the pan once melted.

Test to see if the oil is hot enough by dropping in a little bit of the batter. If it starts to float right away and become golden, then it is ready.

Use a tablespoon to drop batter into the frying pan. Usually, I can get about 5 pancakes in the pan at a time, depending on how large my pan is. When the bottom of the pancakes start to become golden, flip to fry the other side.

Once both sides of the pancakes are golden brown, place them onto a platter lined with paper towels to help absorb the excess oil. Serve right away with jelly.

Tips

- You can use other oils for frying. But according to my mom, if you fry these in anything else besides shortening, they won't be as good. I tried coconut oil, and she did not approve.
- The batter should be slightly thinner than regular pancake batter. If it seems too thick, add some more milk; if it's too thin, add some more flour.
- These are small pancakes, but they are supposed to be that way. I do not recommend making these the size of a regular pancake.
- My mom always uses a fork to flip the pancakes. You can use tongs as well. Either of those options is better than using a spatula.
- We like to combine the flavors of currant and raspberry together by mixing 3/4 cup currant jelly with 1/4 cup raspberry jelly.

CHOCOLATE PEANUT BUTTER BONBONS

Chocolate and peanut butter is a match made in heaven. But these little bites are not the "buckeyes" that you may be used to seeing. Rice cereal gives them a perfect crunch, and they are fully dipped in chocolate to make them completely coated and so craveable. This recipe is from my mom's side, and it was always my absolute favorite during Christmastime. I have made these for some of the most significant moments in my life, including bringing them to producers and cast members the first time I ever had a shot to come onto Hallmark Channel's *Home & Family* show. I put together boxes of these perfect little treats, and it was this recipe that got me asked back to come into the kitchen on the show to make them for a second segment. The rest, as they say, is history!

MAKES 45 TO 50 BONBONS

1/2 cup unsalted butter, room temperature

2 cups peanut butter

1 pound powdered sugar

3 cups crisp rice cereal

1 pound candy coating chocolate (I like milk chocolate or dark chocolate)

Stir the butter and peanut butter together in the bowl of a stand mixer with a paddle attachment. With the mixer on low, slowly add the powdered sugar. Add in the rice cereal and mix until well combined.

Scoop tablespoon-size amounts of the mixture and place on a baking sheet lined with wax paper. Use your hands to roll the scooped mixture into smooth balls and place back onto the wax paper. Refrigerate for at least 2 hours.

Once the mixture is chilled, melt the chocolate by placing it in a bowl over a pot of simmering water (or a double boiler), being careful the water isn't touching the bowl.

Use a fork to dip the cold bonbons into the melted chocolate. Roll the bonbons around to coat them, working quickly.

Scoop the bonbons out with the fork, then tap the fork on the side of the bowl to remove excess chocolate. Place the bonbons on a sheet of wax paper to set.

Tips

- Use a cookie scoop to make the bonbons uniform in size.
- Drizzle melted chocolate over the bonbons once they're set by either using a piping bag or letting the chocolate drip off the back of a spoon.
- If you want to add sprinkles to the top of the bonbon, do this immediately after the bonbon is dipped, before the chocolate starts to harden.

Tips: Create Memories

Get creative. Your family recipes don't have to be anything too elaborate or crazy. They can be a special way you make grilled cheese, or that seasoning you *always* use that sets a certain recipe over the top.

Make it a tradition. Consistency is key when it comes to making memories. Whether it's something you make every week, every Christmas, or "only for special occasions," traditions exemplify specialness and consistency. I've said it once and I'll say it again: traditions are the foundations for memories, and family recipes are all about the memories.

Store your recipes and get your family favorites. My prized possessions are the cookbooks created by Grandpa Provenzano, in his handwriting, and the cookbooks filled with family recipes my mom put together for our family. Passing down recipes is so special. It's heartwarming to know that you are smelling the same smells and tasting the same flavors that your great-grandparents did. One day, when I have grandchildren and great-grandchildren, I want them to know how special these recipes are and have the same experience my family had with them.

FRIENDS
+ WINE =
EVERYTHING'S
FINE

A night with good friends, good food, and good wine is the best form of therapy. Sometimes we just need to be surrounded by the people who will make us laugh so hard our faces hurt, listen to our problems so we don't feel like we are alone, and reminisce about crazy life experiences. Wine nights with my friends always leave me feeling comforted because creating a supportive community is what friendship is all about, and celebrating that together over food and wine will make everything fine!

Set the Scene

You don't have to be a sommelier to learn about wine. The art of wine is fascinating and can lead to stimulating conversation among friends. I love the idea of picking a theme and having everyone bring a bottle for tasting. This could be done by the location (Italian wine, French wine, California wine, etc.), the grape (pinot noir, sauvignon blanc, merlot, chardonnay, etc.), or simply the color of wine (red or white). This menu happens to be geared more toward an Italian-themed night. (Imagine that.)

Since you are with your friends, you don't need to get too fancy! Make it comfortable and fun. I use the same food-grade butcher paper that I use for Making Messes Monday so that I can set out the food and label the dishes on the paper. Give each guest a pen and encourage them to write down tasting notes on the paper. Craft an experience your gang will never forget by lighting candles and adding a smooth Spotify playlist to the mix. And because La Gioiosa Prosecco is not only party-friendly but also food-friendly, it's perfect to enjoy with friends and snacks.[*]

Bonus tip: make sure that everything you are decorating with is scentless so it doesn't compete with the smell of the wine. Cheers! Or shall I say, *"Cin cin!"*

---

[*] Sponsored product; see author's note on page ix.

Tasting Notes

WINE GLASS TAGS

It's a great idea to have something memorable to do at the beginning of the party. Making wine tags is perfect because everyone can put them either on their glasses or on the bottle of wine they brought.

MAKES 1 TAG

Oven-bake clay in a variety of colors

Cutting board

Craft rolling pin

Small circle cookie cutter, optional

Small letter stamps for clay

Toothpick or straw

Baking sheet

Parchment paper

Twine

Work the clay between your hands to soften it a bit. Place the clay onto the cutting board and use a rolling pin to flatten it out to about 1/4 inch thick.

Cut out a circle with a cookie cutter. Press the letter stamp gently onto the circle to create an indentation with the letter. Use the toothpick or straw to create a hole at the top of the circle big enough for the twine to fit through after the clay bakes.

Place the prepared circle of clay onto a baking sheet lined with parchment paper. Bake according to package instructions. Allow the clay to cool completely.

String the twine through the hole and tie onto your wine glass.

Tips

- Sprinkle a bit of cornstarch onto the board to help prevent the clay from sticking to the board.
- If you do not have letter stamps, you can use a permanent marker to write on the clay once it is baked and cooled.
- These can be in other shapes besides circles. Use additional cookie cutters or a craft knife to create other shapes.

WHITE WINE ARTICHOKES

Artichokes are one of my favorite foods, but I have to tell you, I really do not like going through the process of cutting them and scooping the inside out. I have a secret: I buy frozen artichokes. I always have them in my freezer because I love adding them to pizzas and pastas. Artichokes feel fancy, so this is the perfect recipe to kick off your wine night.

MAKES 4 SERVINGS

16 ounces frozen quartered artichoke hearts

4 tablespoons olive oil, divided, plus more for topping

1 teaspoon salt, divided

1 large (or 2 small) thinly sliced shallots

1 garlic clove, minced

1/2 cup dry white wine

4 tablespoons unsalted butter

1/4 cup chopped fresh parsley

1 lemon cut into wedges

2 to 3 sprigs fresh thyme for topping

Defrost the artichokes in a strainer. Once defrosted, pat with a paper towel to remove any additional moisture.

Heat 2 tablespoons of olive oil in a medium skillet over medium-high heat. Place the artichokes into the skillet with about half of the salt and cook until the sides start to brown.

Remove the artichokes from the skillet and place in a separate bowl.

Add the remaining 2 tablespoons of olive oil to the skillet and add in the shallots with the remaining 1/2 teaspoon of salt. Cook until the shallots start to soften. Stir in the garlic and cook until fragrant, about 30 seconds. Add the wine and bring to a boil, then reduce to a simmer.

Cook the wine down until it reduces, about 5 to 7 minutes.

Whisk in the butter 1 tablespoon at a time, making sure each tablespoon mixes in before adding the next one. Add the artichokes and simmer in the sauce for about 5 to 10 minutes.

Pour the artichokes and sauce onto a serving platter and sprinkle the parsley over the artichokes. Serve with lemon wedges and top with sprigs of fresh thyme.

Tips

- Serve the artichokes with fresh bread like an Italian focaccia or a French baguette.
- Using a dry white keeps the flavors light.
- If you need to keep the artichokes warm while preparing other food, place them on an oven-safe platter in a warm oven (about 170 degrees).

CHEESE-STUFFED MEATBALLS WITH RED WINE TOMATO SAUCE

Did you know that in Italy meatballs are not served with pasta? That's more of an Italian American custom. We are going to pretend we are in Italy by serving these meatballs solo with a lovely red wine tomato sauce. I like to fill the meatballs with a smoky mozzarella that not only adds depth of flavor but makes these meatballs so tender.

MAKES 60 MEATBALLS
(8 TO 10 SERVINGS)

2 to 3 tablespoons olive oil

1 onion, finely chopped

1 teaspoon salt, divided

4 garlic cloves, minced

1/4 teaspoon dried rosemary

1/2 teaspoon dried basil

1 teaspoon dried oregano

2/3 cup plain bread crumbs

3/4 cup chopped fresh parsley

1 cup freshly grated Parmesan cheese

2 large eggs, room temperature

1/4 cup ketchup

1/4 cup half-and-half (or cream or whole milk), room temperature

1/4 teaspoon pepper

1 pound ground beef

1 pound ground pork

6 ounces smoked mozzarella cheese

Preheat the oven to 400 degrees.

Heat the olive oil in a medium skillet over medium heat; add the onions with a sprinkle of salt, and cook until the onions are softened. Add the garlic, rosemary, basil, and oregano. Cook for another 30 seconds or until fragrant, being careful not to brown the garlic. Transfer to a large bowl and allow to cool.

In another bowl, combine the bread crumbs, parsley, and Parmesan.

In a small bowl, whisk the eggs together. Add the eggs to the cooled onion mixture, then stir in the ketchup, half-and-half, remaining salt, and pepper.

Add the ground beef and pork. Start mixing by breaking the meat up with a fork, then use your hands to combine the mixture, being careful not to overmix.

Use a small scoop or tablespoon measuring spoon to place the meatballs onto baking sheets lined with aluminum foil. This will make about 60 small meatballs, so you will need 2 or 3 baking sheets.

Cut the mozzarella into cubes small enough to fit inside the scooped meatballs. Use your finger to poke a hole in the center of each meatball. Place one cube of smoked mozzarella in each hole. Cover and roll the meatballs into round shapes. Place the stuffed meatballs back onto the baking sheet.

Bake the meatballs for 10 to 15 minutes or until cooked through.

RED WINE TOMATO SAUCE

MAKES 8 TO 10 SERVINGS

1/4 cup olive oil

1 garlic clove, smashed

1/2 cup dry red wine

1 (28-ounce) can crushed tomatoes

1 (28-ounce) can diced tomatoes

1/2 teaspoon dried basil

1/2 teaspoon dried rosemary

1/2 teaspoon dried oregano

Freshly chopped basil and parsley

Heat the olive oil in a large pot over medium heat. Place the smashed garlic clove into the pot and allow it to cook for a couple minutes until fragrant, moving it around with a wooden spoon to ensure it doesn't brown. Pour in the dry red wine; it will bubble up. Then remove the garlic clove.

Add the crushed tomatoes and the diced tomatoes, along with the basil, rosemary, and oregano; stir to combine.

Bring the sauce to a boil, then reduce to a simmer and allow it to cook for about an hour.

Add Cheese-Stuffed Meatballs to the sauce and cook together for about 20 minutes.

Top with freshly chopped basil and parsley.

Tips

- If using a slow cooker to serve, you can reheat the meatballs in the slow cooker over high heat for about an hour, making sure to stir them every so often until heated through. Then turn the heat to the "warm" setting.
- Serve the meatballs on their own or over pasta (I won't judge).
- Smoked mozzarella is recommended for this recipe; however, plain mozzarella can be used.

ANGEL FOOD CAKE TRIFLE IN A WINE GLASS

This dessert combines two of my absolute favorites: angel food cake and zabaglione. My mom would make angel food cake for my birthday and my dad's birthday every year because it's our favorite cake. Now, you may be asking, what is zabaglione? It's an Italian custard that is usually poured over fruit for dessert. I love the idea of finishing our wine night with a dessert that celebrates wine; zabaglione has Marsala wine, which is a Sicilian fortified wine. It's sweet and has a lovely nutty, caramel flavor to it. Layer the components together in a pretty little wine glass with fresh fruit to create one of my most cherished desserts. (photo page 171)

MAKES ABOUT 12 SERVINGS

1 cup cake flour

1 cup powdered sugar

1/4 teaspoon fine salt

12 large egg whites, room temperature

3/4 cup superfine sugar

1 1/2 teaspoons cream of tartar

1 1/2 teaspoons vanilla extract

Preheat the oven to 350 degrees. Have an ungreased angel food cake pan ready.

In a large bowl, sift together the flour, powdered sugar, and salt. Sift the mixture again to remove any remaining lumps.

Using a stand mixer with the whisk attachment, beat the egg whites on medium speed until they start to foam up.

Separate the superfine sugar into thirds; in one of the thirds, mix in the cream of tartar.

Add one-third of the superfine sugar to the mixer and beat until the egg whites are opaque.

Add the one-third of the superfine sugar that is mixed with the cream of tartar and continue mixing. When the whites start to increase in volume, add the last one-third of the superfine sugar and the vanilla extract, and increase the speed to medium-high. Mix just until the whites form soft peaks; do not overbeat. (If the whites "break," they have been beaten too much.) Remove the bowl from the mixer.

Sift one-third of the dry ingredients over the egg whites and carefully fold the ingredients in with a large spatula. Sift and fold in the remaining dry ingredients in 2 additions, folding in each time. Pour the batter into the pan and smooth the top.

Bake for 40 to 45 minutes or until the top is browned and feels springy when touched. A skewer inserted into the center of the cake should come out clean. Check it around 35 minutes to be safe.

Remove the cake from the oven. If the pan being used has "feet" on it, flip it over and allow it to cool while inverted. If the pan does not have feet, invert it over the neck of a bottle of wine or on top of a can. (I know it sounds crazy, but the cake needs to cool upside down.) Let cool completely.

Tap the pan on the counter to release the cake, then invert it. If the cake does not come out easily, run a thin-bladed knife around the outer sides of the pan and around the inside of the tube.

Serve the cake by placing it on a cake platter and sprinkling with powdered sugar, or cut it into small pieces for a trifle.

If making a trifle, cut the cake into 1-inch pieces with a serrated knife and layer them into a wine glass with fruit and either zabaglione or fresh whipped cream.

ZABAGLIONE

12 egg yolks

1 cup sugar

1/2 cup Marsala wine

Create a double boiler by setting a saucepan of water on the stove and bringing it to a simmer.

In a glass bowl that fits on top of the saucepan but doesn't touch the simmering water, whisk together the egg yolks and sugar until pale yellow and creamy.

Set the bowl on top of the pot of simmering water. Add Marsala and continue to whisk until the mixture starts to thicken to a pourable custard consistency. Serve warm.

Tips

- Make sure the bowl and whisk you are using for the angel food cake are cleaned well, as excess oils can prevent the eggs from whipping up nicely. I clean mine with white vinegar and a paper towel.
- Angel food cake is fragile, so always cut it with a serrated knife or a cutter meant specifically for angel food cakes.
- You can also serve this dessert simply by cutting the cake into slices with a serrated knife and topping each slice with a spoonful of the zabaglione and fresh fruit.

Tips: Grazing Boards

Charcuterie boards can feel extravagant, but they require only a few basic steps. Think color, texture, and balance of flavors.

Start with the board. I recommend using a wood cutting board. It creates a rustic feel and makes the cheese easy to slice.

Choose three different types of cheese. This is a good rule of thumb because then you check off all the boxes for what people like. Choose one from each of the following categories:

- Soft: Brie, goat, burrata
- Firm: Parmesan, cheddar, Gruyère, Gouda
- Pungent: Stilton, Roquefort, Gorgonzola

Use the right cheese knives. Each cheese should have its own knife—and be sure it slices the cheese well. For instance, the soft cheese will need a knife that is good for spreading, and the firm cheese will need a knife that is sharp enough to slice through it.

Add fruit for sweetness. I tend to use dried fruit in evening events and fresh fruit during morning or afternoon events. You can use either or both. Consider mixing in the following:

- Dried: cherries, apricots, figs, dates
- Fresh: strawberries, grapes, raspberries, blueberries, melon, pears, apricots

Put nuts on the side. Nuts are great for a touch of crunch. However, they can be an issue for those with allergies. I recommend putting nuts—such as walnuts, Marcona almonds, or hazelnuts—in a separate bowl to play it safe.

Consider olives for a salty bite. Place the olives in a separate bowl, instead of directly onto the cutting board, because of the oils. Pitted olives are your best option so that everyone isn't spitting out pits. I recommend buying marinated olives that are a mix of black and green.

Go for cured meats. These add a savory balance to a charcuterie board. I recommend two types of meat. Choose from options such as prosciutto, salami, and spicy soppressata.

Top it off with crackers. It isn't a cheese board without the crackers. I'm a carb lover, so I usually do three kinds of crackers, but you need only two: one that is more buttery and crumbly and one that is more salty and crunchy.

Don't overcrowd the platter. There are many great photos of charcuterie platters that are packed to the brim, but be sure each item has enough space.

Outsource! Guests always ask what they can bring, and this is the perfect menu feature to have your guests help with. Either outsource the entire board or have everyone bring a couple of items and assemble it together.

---

* Sponsored product; see author's note on page ix.

BOOKS-OPTIONAL BOOK CLUB

I love everything about my book club—the stories, the conversation, the wine, and the moments spent with those people I adore. Book clubs are a great way to bring friends together to chat about something different from the usual work/kids/life conversation. I think we can forget how lovely it is to sit in a cozy chair, have a little peace and quiet, and get lost in a great book. The idea sounds great but isn't always attainable, so at my book club, the books are optional—encouraged, but optional. No one gets detention at my book club! I like to invite everyone to get together without feeling like it's an assignment. If someone in the group doesn't get around to reading the book, then everyone else can share the story with them. Book clubs are about getting together with your friends and celebrating the art of storytelling, even if that means you end up telling one another a story or two about your kids. Host a book club and enjoy food, wine, and togetherness.

*   Sponsored product; see author's note on page ix.

Set the Scene

If you haven't noticed, I'm a sucker for a good theme! Book club parties are perfect for that.

Dive into the narrative of whatever book you're reading to use as a guide for your theme. For example, if you're reading a novel set in the English countryside, break out the lace doilies and set out your tea set. Let the book you're reading inspire your decorating. You can also celebrate the written word by decorating with books! Books from your local antiques store make for a vintage look. Layer the books on top of one another and top them with a small vase of flowers or candles. This adds depth, dimension, and creativity to your table.

CUSTOM BOOKMARKS

My son Grant made me an absolutely adorable bookmark at school. He was beaming with pride when he gave it to me. I melted; it was just too cute. He inspired me to come up with this idea for a bookmark that is pretty, customizable, and sturdy. These make lovely gifts for a book club celebration.

MAKES 1 BOOKMARK

Silicone bookmark mold

Baking sheet

Liquid clay in a variety of colors

Toothpick

Tassel for decoration

Place the silicone mold onto the baking sheet. Fill the mold with the liquid clay. Use a toothpick, if needed, to help get the clay into the corners and around the top where the hole is.

Bake according to package directions and allow to cool completely.

Add additional decor, such as name labels, if desired. Add a tassel or ribbon through the hole at the top to finish off the bookmark.

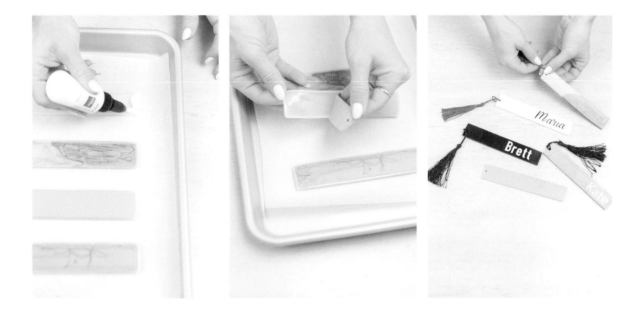

Tips

- Use a cutting machine to create vinyl letters or a paint pen to add lettering to the bookmarks.
- Use multiple colors of liquid clay and swirl them together with a toothpick to create a marbled look.
- For an extra sparkle, add some glitter with a thin layer of Mod Podge. Let it dry completely, then seal the glitter in with another layer of Mod Podge.

PESTO, GOAT CHEESE, AND TOMATO CROSTINI

With all this book discussion, you and your guests are going to work up quite the appetite. Here come the crostini to the rescue! This recipe is my go-to appetizer for just about any celebration. It pairs well with my favorite everyday Prosecco by La Gioiosa DOC and is a lovely way to kick off the friendship celebration.*

MAKES 4 TO 6 SERVINGS

1 baguette

4 tablespoons olive oil

4 to 6 ounces goat cheese

Lemony Basil Pesto (page 51)

1 pint fresh tomatoes

Salt (preferably sea salt or kosher salt)

Turn the oven to broil.

Slice the baguette on an angle, about $\frac{1}{2}$ to 1 inch thick. Drizzle the olive oil on both sides of the bread so that each side is evenly covered; using a pastry brush can help.

Place the bread onto a baking sheet lined with aluminum foil and bake in the oven until the edges start to become slightly golden.

Remove the baking sheet from the oven and flip the pieces over. Place the baking sheet back into the oven and allow the other side of the bread to become lightly golden as well. This happens quickly; don't take your eyes off it.

Remove the baking sheet from the oven and let the bread cool enough to touch.

Spread a thin layer of goat cheese onto the bread. Spread a teaspoon or so of the pesto over the goat cheese on each piece. Slice the tomatoes into thin slices and place them on the pesto.

Sprinkle with a small amount of salt to taste.

Tips

- Place the rack in the oven toward the top closer to the broiler.
- Grilling the bread is another option. If the weather is nice, having an outdoor book club with freshly grilled crostini would be lovely!
- Make sure not to make the bread too crunchy by cooking it for too long.

---

* Sponsored product; see author's note on page ix.

CRUNCHY BOWL SALAD BITES

This is no ordinary salad, mind you; this salad acts like an appetizer. These little salad bowls made from Parmesan cheese add a salty crunch when you bite into them. They are also easy to eat and easy to pass around, and they don't require a fork. Tell me another salad that can do that! These tasty appetizers are delicious and will keep everyone chatting chapter after chapter.

MAKES 12 SALAD BITES

12 tablespoons freshly grated
Parmesan cheese

Muffin tin

2 cups salad greens

Simple Salad Dressing (page 183)

Preheat the oven to 350 degrees. Line a half-sheet baking pan with parchment paper or a Silpat sheet.

Scoop 1 tablespoon of Parmesan into a mound onto the prepared pan and spread it around so that it is roughly a 3-inch flat circle. Leave 2-inch gaps between your rounds. You can fit 6 rounds onto each baking sheet.

Bake for about 10 to 12 minutes or until bubbly and lightly golden.

Remove the pan from the oven and use an offset spatula, or knife, to place the cheese rounds into the muffin tin molds. Push the cheese round in so that it will hold the indentation in the center. Allow the cheese to cool in this shape.

Once the cheese has cooled, fill with salad and dressing and serve.

SIMPLE SALAD DRESSING

MAKES ABOUT 1 1/2 CUPS

7 tablespoons red wine vinegar

1 tablespoon Dijon mustard

1 garlic clove, minced

1 teaspoon salt

1/2 teaspoon freshly ground
black pepper

1/2 cup olive oil

1/2 cup toasted sunflower oil (or
any other flavor nut or seed oil)

In a blender, combine the vinegar, mustard, garlic, salt, and pepper. Slowly add the olive oil and sunflower oil to blend. Adjust seasonings to taste. For more flavor, add fresh herbs, such as basil or parsley.

The ingredients can also be placed in a mason jar and shaken to mix.

Tips

- I like to grate my cheese in a food processor, as it yields the best results. Grated cheese from the store doesn't work quite as well.
- Work fast as the cheese will harden quickly—but the cheese is hot, so work with caution. I like to make these in batches about 3 to 4 at a time.
- To maintain the crispness of the cheese, fill the cups right before you are ready to serve.

CHOCOLATE BUTTERFLY CUPCAKE TOPPERS AND CHAI TEA LATTE CUPCAKES

My dream reading location involves a comfy blanket, a cozy chair, and a piping hot chai latte. The flavors of a chai latte are infused perfectly in these cupcakes. But I couldn't stop there; since this dessert is to be served at the close of the evening, I had to end with a "wow" factor. These heavenly chai latte cupcakes are topped with a chocolate butterfly. And because I love a good theme, the butterfly shape is created by having the chocolate harden in an open book. How cool is that?

CHOCOLATE BUTTERFLY CAKE TOPPERS

MAKES APPROXIMATELY 12
BUTTERFLY TOPPERS, DEPENDING
ON SIZE

Printed butterfly design, about 4 inches wide (draw or print from online)

Wax paper

Book, at least 1 inch thick

8 ounces chocolate candy melts

Heatproof bowl

Piping bag

Wax paper

Draw or print the butterfly design onto paper and top it with a sheet of wax paper similar in size.

Open the book in the center so that it lies as even and flat as possible.

Place the chocolate in a heatproof bowl and melt according to package instructions, either in the microwave or in a double boiler.

Pour the melted chocolate into a piping bag. Cut the tip off the piping bag, creating just a small hole. Twist the open end of the piping bag with your writing hand to close it up.

Pipe the chocolate over the butterfly design, being careful not to squeeze too hard.

Carefully place the wax paper onto the opened book so that the center of the butterfly is in the center of the book and the wings are on the pages. Allow the chocolate to cool completely, then carefully remove the butterfly from the wax paper and place it on a cupcake.

Tips

- Make sure the book you use is able to stay open and lie flat.
- If you cut too much off the tip of the piping bag, too much chocolate will come out, and it will be difficult to create a design. Avoid this common mistake by cutting only a small amount from the tip of the bag.
- Create different colors and designs on the butterfly with colorful candy melts.
- If you have difficulty with the chocolate running, pipe thinner lines of chocolate.

CHAI TEA LATTE CUPCAKES

MAKES 20 TO 24 CUPCAKES

½ cup whole milk

1 chai tea bag

3 cups all-purpose flour

1 teaspoon baking powder

½ teaspoon baking soda

4 tablespoons Chai Spice Mix (page 187)

½ teaspoon salt

1 cup unsalted butter, room temperature

2 cups sugar

5 large eggs, room temperature

½ cup sour cream, room temperature

½ cup mild-flavor oil, such as sunflower oil, or any other vegetable oil of choice

2 teaspoons vanilla extract

In a small pot, heat the milk to just under a boil. Add the chai tea bag and steep for about 5 to 7 minutes, until the milk is flavored with the tea. Allow the milk to cool to room temperature.

Preheat the oven to 325 degrees. Spray two 12-cup muffin pans with cooking spray or line with cupcake liners.

In a medium bowl, whisk together the flour, baking powder, baking soda, chai spice, and salt. Set aside.

In a stand mixer with a paddle attachment, beat the butter and sugar together on medium-high speed until light and fluffy, about 2 minutes. With the mixer on low, stir in the eggs one at a time until each one is combined. Scrape the sides and bottom of the bowl with a rubber spatula as needed.

Stir the chai-flavored milk, sour cream, oil, and vanilla extract together in a small bowl.

With the mixer on low speed, add in half of the dry ingredients and mix until just combined.

With the mixer still running on low, slowly pour in the chai milk. Stir in the rest of the flour mixture and mix until just combined, being careful not to overmix.

Scoop the batter into the prepared muffin pan.

Bake for 25 to 35 minutes or until a toothpick inserted in the center comes out clean.

Allow the cupcakes to cool completely before frosting.

CHAI SPICE BUTTERCREAM

MAKES 3 CUPS

1 cup unsalted butter

1 pound powdered sugar

1 teaspoon Chai Spice Mix (page 187)

2 teaspoons vanilla extract

2 to 4 tablespoons half-and-half, room temperature, divided

Attach the paddle attachment to a stand mixer and mix the butter on medium speed until softened.

In another medium bowl, whisk together the powdered sugar and Chai Spice Mix.

Slowly add in the powdered dry mixture to the butter mixture with the mixer on low. Stir in the vanilla extract and 2 tablespoons of the half-and-half. Increase the speed to medium-high and mix until the frosting is lighter in texture and has a spreadable consistency, about 2 to 3 minutes.

Add more powdered sugar if the frosting is too thin or more half-and-half if it's too thick.

CHAI SPICE MIX

MAKES APPROXIMATELY
3 TABLESPOONS

4 teaspoons ground cinnamon

2 teaspoons ground cardamom

2 teaspoons ground ginger

1 teaspoon ground allspice

1 teaspoon ground nutmeg

1/2 teaspoon ground cloves

Mix the cinnamon, cardamon, ginger, allspice, nutmeg, and cloves together until combined. Store in an airtight container.

Tips

- Make these into mini cupcakes by using a mini cupcake pan and baking them for about 11 to 13 minutes at the same temperature.
- Sprinkle more of the spice mix onto the finished cupcakes for additional chai spice flavor.

Tips: **Book Club Topics**

Each month, I ask the members to put forward a book they are interested in, and the club votes. Alternatively, each member takes a turn choosing a selection. I love taking everyone's ideas into consideration because it keeps things interesting. Here are some good starting suggestions:

- The classics: *Jane Eyre, Pride and Prejudice*
- The life changers: *The Gratitude Diaries, Big Magic*
- The romantic comedy read: *Meet Cute, Mrs. Everything*

Getting the conversation started can be one of the biggest challenges. That's why I've assembled a list of simple questions to get your group talking:

- Which character did you like or relate to the most? Why?
- If you were making your own movie about this book, who would you cast?
- If you had the chance to ask the author one question, what would you ask?
- Who in your life would you recommend this book to and why?

SELF-CARE
TO SHARE
SPA DAY

Self-care is personal and looks different for each of us. For me, self-care is simply the act of, well, taking care of yourself! That can mean working to protect, support, and improve all aspects of your own health. To some that may mean taking a day off now and then or setting aside time to get a manicure, exercise, or get enough sleep. Whether it's mental, emotional, or physical self-care, it's important.

My self-care includes ample time with my friends. Giving time and energy to my friendships creates the richest reward. Thoughtful interactions or even simply texting memes back and forth can leave me belly laughing. Brunches with my friends leave me feeling like my self-care cup is totally full. Time spent in the presence of these girls adds so much fullness to my life. What better way to celebrate my friendships then with a self-care to share spa day?

Set the Scene

Host a tranquil at-home spa day for your friends that will instantly create a moment of zen. Start by clearing the clutter from a room and adding candles to the space. They smell amazing, offer gentle light, and are so calming. Scatter some tea lights or opt for a floating candle centerpiece. Next, add the power of a calming scent with an oil diffuser. My go-to for a spa vibe is the sweet aroma of lavender because it's instantly relaxing; you could also try the stimulating fragrance of eucalyptus. Give your friends the full spa treatment by setting up beautifying and calming activities and treats. Start with Sparkling Blackberry Mint Water (page 195) for them to sip, face masks, and mani-pedi stations around your space. On the invitation, let them know to arrive in their comfy jammies for a pamper party like no other.

WATERCOLOR SPA BAGS: SUGAR FOOT SCRUB AND BATH MELTS

Canvas bags are a perfect blank . . . canvas. For a friend's bachelorette weekend, I made the bags ahead of time and filled them with goodies because we went on a trip and everyone carried around the bags the entire weekend. For a spa day, I love that the party favors can double as a great DIY to do together. I recommend having a sample already made so that everyone has an idea of what to do. I also place the additional party favors that go in the bag on the same table or nearby so everyone knows to fill their bags at the end of the party.

WATERCOLOR BAG SUPPLIES

MAKES 1 BAG

Magazines to go inside each bag

Canvas bags

Pencil

Paintbrush

Water

Fabric paint

GIFTS FOR INSIDE THE BAGS

Nail file

Nail polish

Headband and scrunchie

Sugar Scrub (page 193)

Bath Melts (page 194)

Work on a covered surface. Place a magazine inside the canvas bag to prevent the paint from bleeding through to the other side.

Use a pencil to lightly draw or trace your design.

Dip your paintbrush in the water, then in the paint, and start your design. It helps to dip into the water frequently to create the watercolor look and to help the color spread.

Allow the canvas bags to dry, then fill with whatever gifts you like!

SUGAR SCRUB

MAKES ABOUT 2 1/2 CUPS

2 cups white sugar

1/2 cup coconut oil

2 tablespoons olive oil

A few drops of rose essential oil, if desired

Petals from 2 roses

Place the sugar, coconut oil, olive oil, and essential oil (if desired) in a food processor and process until smooth. Add the rose petals and pulse a few times to gently mix.

Package in glass jars with lids and use within a few weeks. Store at room temperature.

BATH MELTS

1/3 cup shea butter

1/3 cup avocado oil

1/4 cup honey

Heatproof bowl

2 cups powdered milk, divided

Cookie scoop

Wax sheet

Place the shea butter, avocado oil, and honey into a heat-proof bowl. Place the bowl over a pot with simmering water to create a double boiler and heat the mixture until just melted.

Allow to cool a bit, then add 1 cup of the powdered milk. If the mixture is still too runny, add more powdered milk, up to 1/2 cup.

Scoop the mixture using a cookie scoop if you want the bath melts to be similar in size, about 1 1/2 tablespoons each. Use your hands to roll the mixture into a ball and place it on a wax sheet to set up.

Roll in extra powdered milk to make the balls look more finished and pretty. Package them in a bag or container, but be sure to wrap them individually so they do not stick together.

To use, fill a bath with hot water and place the bath melt into the bath; use your hands to swirl the water until the melt dissolves.

Tip

▪ After the bath, the oils remain on the skin, but it helps to rinse quickly to remove any excess milk from your skin. Your skin will feel soft and moisturized.

SPARKLING BLACKBERRY MINT WATER

Spas usually serve water infused with a lovely blend of fruit and herbs—so refreshing! Since we're bringing the serenity of the spa home, I thought I'd add my spin on this thirst-quenching beverage. Adding sparkling water to this elixir provides the effervescence I love, and poured over ice, it makes for the perfect mocktail. Hydrate as you elevate your mental state with this crisp, cool concoction. (photo page 188)

MAKES ONE DRINK

Ice

Blackberries

Mint

Sparkling water, cold

Simple syrup, optional

Fill a tall glass halfway with ice.

Add 3 to 4 blackberries and 2 to 3 mint leaves, depending on your preference.

Fill the cup with sparkling water.

Make a simple syrup by boiling equal parts sugar and water together until the sugar has dissolved. Allow the mixture to cool completely. Add simple syrup to taste.

Tips

- Create these drinks individually for the best bubbles. There is nothing worse than a flat drink that is supposed to be bubbly.
- Make sure the sparkling water is cold. Either keep it in the fridge or use an ice bucket.
- Provide a variety of fruit and herbs and display them by the drinks so people have options to choose from.
- Decorate with the herbs, but don't go crazy. Herbs can have a very strong smell and, depending on your space, could overwhelm the smell of the room.

SPA CITRUS AND BURRATA SALAD "ITALIANO"

One of my favorite recipes in my grandpa's cookbook is a recipe for a light and refreshing citrus salad that includes full segments of lemon along with grapefruit and oranges. I created a recipe inspired by Grandpa, but instead of the lemon pieces, I squeezed some lemon juice over the top to finish, added some sweetness with a little honey, and added an herbaceous touch with basil and mint. I decided to make it extra special for our spa theme with luxurious burrata and edible flowers. This dish is almost too pretty to eat. (Almost.)

SERVES 4

2 grapefruits

2 oranges

2 (8-ounce) balls of burrata

1/3 cup chopped mint

1/3 cup chopped or torn basil

Edible flowers, optional

Olive oil to taste

Honey to taste

Sea salt to taste

Pepper to taste, optional

Cut the grapefruit and oranges by cutting off the outer peel and the pith. Cut the fruit into 1/4- to 1/2-inch pieces, or segment the grapefruit and the oranges by using a knife to cut off the peel, then use a small, sharp knife to cut between each segment to remove the pieces of the fruit.

Place the burrata onto a platter and use your hands to break it up into smaller pieces.

Place the cut grapefruit and oranges around the burrata. Sprinkle the mint and basil over the citrus and burrata. Place the edible flowers around the platter.

Lightly drizzle olive oil and honey over the top and then sprinkle with sea salt and pepper to taste. Adjust the flavors and add more of anything you like.

Tips

- For a kick, I like to add thinly sliced red onion.
- The fruit can be cut ahead of time and stored in a sealed container in the fridge until ready to assemble on the platter.
- Not everyone likes pepper on fruit, but I happen to love it. I promise it's worth a try.
- Mix up the citrus as needed and use what's in season. Blood oranges would taste great, or add other fruit like peaches or strawberries.

MAKE-AHEAD TEA SANDWICHES THREE WAYS

Food at a spa is light, refreshing, and easy to eat. Tea sandwiches are lovely because you can make a variety of options to meet any dietary needs, from vegans to meat lovers. You can get as creative as you like or keep these as simple as you like. The key is to add lots of color and texture, and to cut the sandwiches into bite-sized pieces. (photo pages 198–99)

CUCUMBER AND CRÈME FRAÎCHE

MAKES APPROXIMATELY
8 SANDWICHES

1 English cucumber
4 ounces crème fraîche
1 tablespoon minced chives
Salt and pepper to taste
4 slices soft white bread
1 lemon, cut into wedges

Use a knife to cut off the ends of the cucumber. Use a mandoline or a sharp knife to carefully cut the cucumber into very thin rounds.

In a small bowl, mix together the crème fraîche, chives, and salt and pepper until well combined.

Apply a layer of the crème fraîche to the bread slices. Place the cucumber onto the bread in a uniform way. Stack one of the pieces onto another, both with the cucumber facing up.

Use a sharp knife to cut off the crusts and create an even square of bread. Cut the square into four quarters by first cutting down the center to create two rectangles, and then cut those rectangles in half. This will create 4 stacked sandwiches. These can also be served without stacking.

Add a squeeze of lemon over the top and an additional sprinkle of salt if needed.

SMOKED SALMON AND AVOCADO AND DILL

MAKES APPROXIMATELY 8
STACKED SANDWICHES OR 16
OPEN-FACE SANDWICHES

1 large avocado
1 lemon, divided, plus more if needed
4 large slices pumpernickel bread
4 to 6 thin slices smoked salmon (amount depends on the size of the slices)
1 tablespoon fresh dill, lightly chopped
Sea salt to taste

Cut the avocado in half and remove the pit. Scoop the inside of the avocado into a small bowl, then use a fork to smash it until a smooth texture is achieved. Squeeze in the juice of half the lemon, and stir together.

Place two pieces of bread on a cutting board and apply a generous layer of the smashed avocado onto them. Top each piece with the salmon. Sprinkle the dill evenly over each piece along with another squeeze of fresh lemon juice and a sprinkle of sea salt to taste. Cover with the other two slices of bread to create sandwiches.

Use a sharp knife to cut the crusts off to create a square. Cut the square into four quarters by first cutting down the center to create two rectangles, and then cut those rectangles in half.

RADISH AND BUTTER

MAKES APPROXIMATELY
8 TO 10 SANDWICHES

1 small baguette, fresh

1/2 cup unsalted butter (preferably European-style), room temperature

1 small bunch of radishes, cleaned and dried

Sea salt to taste

1 small bunch of watercress, washed and dried

Cut the baguette into slices about 1/2 inch thick.

Apply a generous layer of butter onto each slice and place onto a platter.

Use a mandoline or very sharp knife to thinly slice the radishes. Place the cut radishes as generously as you like onto the slices of bread.

Sprinkle with sea salt to taste. Add a piece or two of watercress on top of each slice.

Tips: Spa Towels at Home and DIY Face Mist

Warm towels are one of my favorite things about going to the spa. For my spa day at home, I wanted to create that same pampering feeling—and I'm doing it in a slow cooker. Yes, you heard me right! Depending on the size of your slow cooker, add around 2 cups of water to the bottom of the bowl. Spray small hand towels with a light, naturally scented face mist (like my Aloe and Rosewater Face Mist), roll the towels, and place them into the water. Add another cup or two of water over the towels and set to the "warm" setting. Give them a little time to warm up—about 30 minutes or so. Wrap one of these over your eyes and feel the stresses of the day wash away.

DIY ALOE AND ROSEWATER FACE MIST

MAKES 1 BOTTLE OF SPRAY

1 (2-ounce) spray bottle and mini funnel; usually these will come in kits together

1 ounce 100 percent natural aloe

1/2 ounce rosewater

1 teaspoon jojoba oil

Remove the sprayer part of the bottle and place the mini funnel onto the top.

Pour in the aloe, rosewater, and jojoba oil.

Place the sprayer back on and shake to combine.

Shake well before each use.

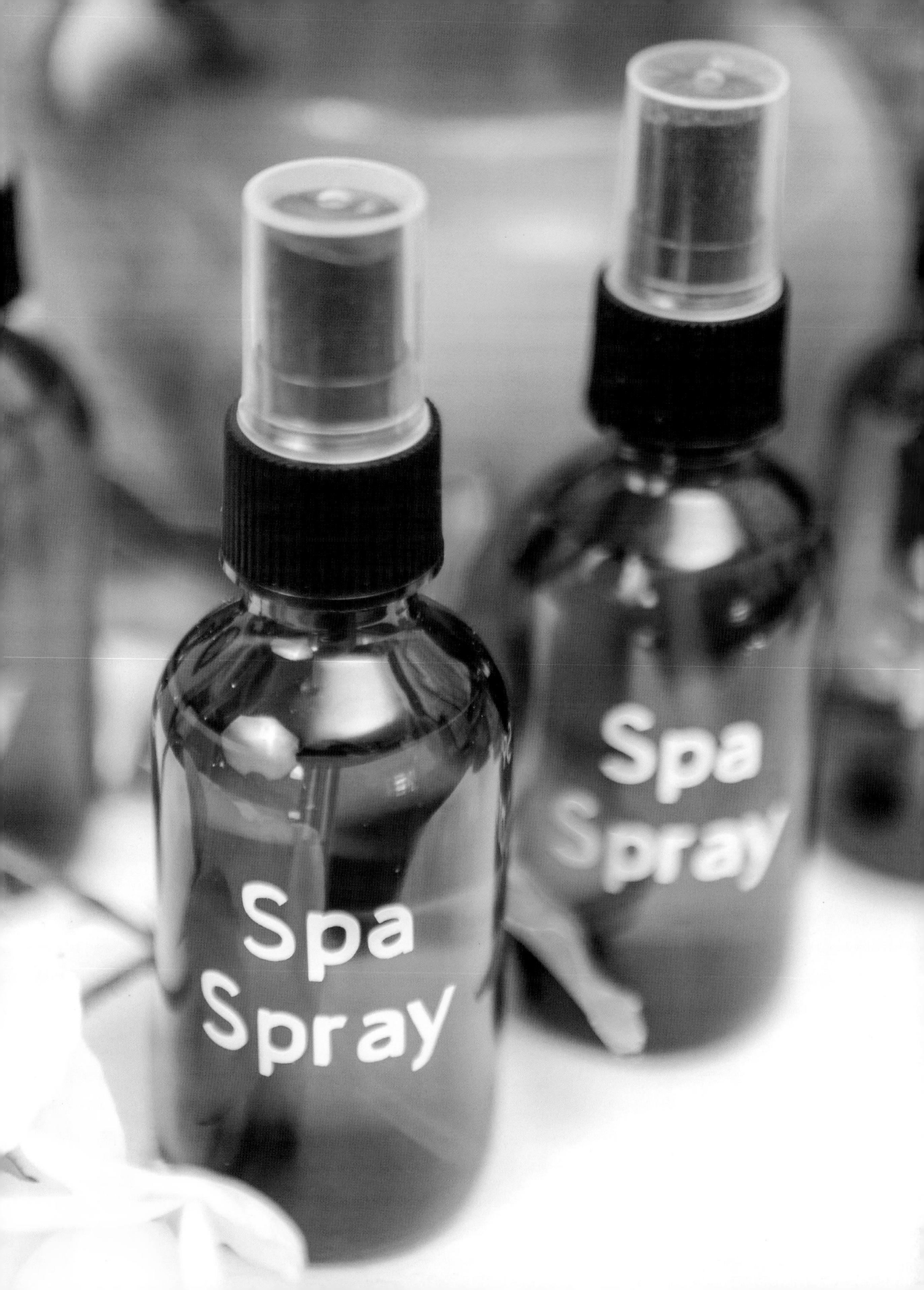
Spa
Spray
Spa
Spray

"FOREVER FRIENDS" SUPPORT

I am so fortunate to be able to count on a select group of amazing ladies I call my "forever friends." We've known each other since before we could walk in heels; we've been there for each other through the great times and the challenging ones.

There is something so special about tried-and-true friends. They're the ones you told about your husband when he was just a first date, the friends you confided in when you had to go through all those frogs to get to your prince, and the girls you can sit with on the couch in your sweats while bingeing on junk food and talking the night away.

And when we're faced with things that we find hard to imagine, those friends are there. They are the support system that makes sure there is a dinner miraculously in the fridge or a basket of treats at the door. They're the ones who pick up your dry cleaning and hang it your closet. They're there when you need them most or when you just need a smile.

Honoring our friends isn't about getting them something with a big price tag but about sharing with them the little things that strengthen already-strong bonds and remind us of why we are so close to begin with. So here's to our "forever friends" and the phenomenal ways they touch our lives.

Set the Scene

When a friend needs some support, comfort is key. Grab a pretty basket and fill it with goodies your friend will love that will provide inspiration, peace, and calm: chocolates and yummy baked goods, something from the savory side of the aisle, or bath and beauty treats. You know your pals, and you know what will make their day a little brighter. Trust yourself and know that when your friend is looking at what you've sent their way, they will be filled with the warmth of friendship. The gift of a true friend is something you can't buy in any store.

COMFORT CANDLE

Candles are such a source of comfort for me. When I need to relax by either taking a nice long bath or sitting in a quiet spot and journaling, lighting a candle always gets me in the right mindset. Candles are a great gift to give friends who need additional support because they're not only getting the benefits the candle provides but also are reminded of your friendship and encouragement.

MAKES 1 LARGE BATCH OF
CANDLES (AMOUNT WILL
VARY DEPENDING ON THE
SIZE OF THE CONTAINERS)

1 pound soy wax

Wax-pouring pitcher (a tall aluminum pot specifically for candle making)

Saucepan large enough to hold the pouring pitcher with additional space on the sides

Spatula

Essential oils safe for candle making; about 1 ounce (check the amount each brand recommends)

Candle wicks

8-ounce heatproof containers for the candles (mason jars, mugs, candle making tins, etc.)

Pencils to hold the wicks in place

Additional decor, such as dried/fresh herbs or spices, labels, stickers, etc.

Place the soy wax chips in a pouring pitcher and place the pitcher in a saucepan with simmering water. Melt the wax, stirring frequently with a spatula.

Remove from the heat and allow to cool to about 160 degrees, then stir in the essential oils.

Prepare the wicks by placing them in the desired containers and holding them in place with 2 pencils.

When the wax cools to about 140 degrees, it can be poured into the prepared containers.

Add the additional decorations, such as dried/fresh flowers or spices, if desired. Allow the wax to set overnight.

Trim the wick down to 1/4 inch before lighting.

Tips

- Personalize the candles with a label or vinyl lettering.
- Top with fresh or dried flowers for a feminine, floral finishing touch or spices like cinnamon sticks, star anise, and cardamom pods for a cozy touch.
- Make sure the containers that the wax is being poured into aren't cold, as this can cause them to break with the extreme difference in temperature. You can place the containers on a baking sheet and keep them in the oven set at the lowest temperature until you are ready to pour the wax.

SUPER NUTRITIOUS MAKE-AHEAD SMOOTHIE PACKS

If a friend is going through a rough spot and needs your support, providing meals can take a huge weight off their shoulders. Comfort food can be healthy, too, and these smoothies are proof of that. Stock your friend's freezer with these Super Nutritious Make-Ahead Smoothie Packs to give them the help they need when it comes to making meals at home.

MAKES 1 SMOOTHIE

Freezer bags
Frozen fruit
Permanent marker or label

Fill the freezer bags with the fruit, squeeze out all the air, and label the bags with the date packed.

Smoothie packs should last in the freezer for up to 3 months.

When ready to blend, add 1 to 2 cups of liquid (water, milk, etc.) into the blender along with the ingredients in the bag and blend up.

COMBINATION IDEAS

TROPICAL

- 1 banana, cut into 1-inch pieces
- 1 cup chopped mango
- 1 cup chopped pineapple

BERRY

- 1 banana, cut into 1-inch pieces
- 2 cups mixed berries

NUTTY

- 1 banana, cut into 1-inch pieces
- 4 dates, chopped
- 2 tablespoons nut butter, such as almond or peanut
- 2 teaspoons of cacao powder to make it chocolatey (optional)

GREENS

- 1 cup strawberries
- 1 banana, cut into 1-inch pieces
- 1 cup spinach or chopped kale

PEACHY

- 1 banana, cut into 1-inch pieces
- 1 cup sliced peaches
- 3/4 cup unsweetened 2 percent Greek yogurt

Tip

When packing these up as gifts, make sure to label what is inside the bags and how to prepare the smoothies. Place the frozen bags into a cooler and deliver with additional ice packs.

SINGLE-SERVE CHEESY TURKEY AND KALE STUFFED SHELLS

Lasagna is a classic meal to give when offering support because it can be easily heated up and it feeds a crowd. But what if your friend doesn't need to feed a crowd or doesn't want to be reminded they don't have a crowd to feed? Single-Serve Cheesy Turkey and Kale Stuffed Shells are here to the rescue! These shells are comfort food on a smaller scale. They can be frozen in individual portions and heated up as needed. The stress of what to make for dinner is gone, and the pressure to eat it is low.

MAKES 25 TO 30 SHELLS

1 bunch kale

Salt and pepper to taste

1 to 2 tablespoons olive oil

1/2 large onion, finely chopped

1 garlic clove, minced

1/2 teaspoon fresh rosemary

2 pounds ground turkey

8 ounces mascarpone cheese, room temperature

1/2 cup freshly grated Parmesan cheese, plus more for serving

25 to 30 pasta shells

3 to 4 cups Homemade Marinara Sauce (page 143)

Fresh basil or parsley for topping

Remove the kale from its large, thick stem and chop into large pieces. Place the kale in a large skillet over medium heat with a sprinkle of salt. Cook until the kale is softened and cooked down. Place in a strainer and allow to drain and cool.

Once cooled, place the kale in a cheesecloth or paper towel to squeeze out the excess liquid. Place on a cutting board and chop into smaller pieces.

Heat the olive oil in a large skillet over medium heat. Add the onions and a sprinkle of salt.

Cook until softened, about 5 minutes. Add the garlic and fresh rosemary; cook for about a minute.

Add the ground turkey; use a wooden spoon to break up the turkey so that it is in small, crumbled pieces. Cook until the turkey is cooked through.

Add the kale, mascarpone, and Parmesan. Stir until evenly mixed. If you want to make this ahead of time, this mixture can be cooled and refrigerated.

Preheat the oven to 375 degrees.

Bring a large pot of water to a boil and add enough salt to flavor the water.

Place the shells in the salted boiling water and cook until very al dente, not completely cooked through, and drain.

<u>To cook the pasta in a large batch:</u>
Pour a thin layer of marinara sauce in the bottom of a rimmed baking dish. Stuff each shell with a scoop of the turkey mixture. Place the stuffed shell onto the layer of marinara; repeat until all of the turkey mixture is used.

Pour some of the marinara over the shells. Sprinkle with some extra Parmesan cheese.

Bake at 375 degrees for about 20 minutes or until bubbly and hot.

Heat more of the marinara sauce in a saucepan to have extra for serving.

Allow the shells to cool for a few minutes before serving. Top with more marinara, fresh herbs like basil or parsley, and Parmesan cheese, if desired.

To freeze the pasta individually and allow it to be cooked later:
Place the unbaked shells into an individual-size freezer-safe container. When ready to bake, defrost and place in a small baking dish and bake according to the large-batch directions.

Tips

- The secret to making these shells really tasty is to not overcook the pasta when it's boiling. Cook it so that it is al dente (has some bite to it) and still pretty sturdy. It will cook more in the oven.
- Spinach is a good alternative to using kale.
- Substitute quality store-bought tomato sauce for the homemade marinara or meat sauce.

CLASSIC CHOCOLATE CHIP COOKIES

If you ask my mom what "home" smells like, she will say without hesitation, "The smell of chocolate chip cookies right out of the oven," and she's not wrong. Sometimes just a little bit of something sweet adds that comfort of your childhood days that you can't get from anything else. When sending Classic Chocolate Chip Cookies to your friends for support, you can deliver them hot and fresh out of the oven, or you can freeze them so that your friends can bake them at their leisure. The advantage of providing the frozen cookies is that the recipient can fill their home with the scent of fresh-baked cookies and, even better, make up only a few at a time instead of having an entire batch at once. (photo page 217)

MAKES ABOUT 25 TO 30 COOKIES

1 cup unsalted butter

1/2 cup sugar

1 cup firmly packed brown sugar (I prefer dark)

1 large egg, room temperature

1 teaspoon vanilla extract

2 cups all-purpose flour

1/2 teaspoon baking soda

1/2 teaspoon baking powder

1/2 teaspoon salt

1/2 teaspoon cinnamon

1 1/2 cups chopped chocolate or chocolate chips (dark or semisweet)

Preheat the oven to 350 degrees.

Place the butter in the bowl of a stand mixer with a paddle attachment (or use a hand mixer). Add the sugar and brown sugar, and mix until light and fluffy, making sure to scrape down the sides of the bowl every so often. Stir in the egg and vanilla extract, and mix until well combined.

In a large bowl, whisk together the flour, baking soda, baking powder, salt, and cinnamon.

Slowly pour the flour into the butter mixture and mix until just combined.

Stir in the chocolate until evenly mixed, scraping down the sides of the bowl to make sure everything is incorporated and being careful not to overmix.

Use a cookie scoop or two spoons to scoop the dough onto a baking sheet lined with parchment paper, spacing the cookies at least a couple of inches away from one another. You can make the cookies any size; I use about 1 heaping tablespoon of dough per cookie.

Bake for 8 to 10 minutes, adjusting the baking time according to size, until the edges start to become golden.

Place the baking sheet on a rack to cool for a couple of minutes. Then remove the parchment paper from the baking sheet and place onto a cooling rack to allow the cookies to cool completely.

Tips

- Use room-temperature ingredients to incorporate everything evenly.
- Mix the butter and sugar together until the mixture is light and fluffy. This can take a few minutes.
- Try using chopped chocolate instead of chocolate chips. It has a more gourmet texture and distributes chocolate throughout the batter so that it is in every bite.
- Don't overmix once you add the flour. Overmixing creates tough cookies.
- I like using a cookie scoop when making cookies so they are uniform in size and bake evenly.
- Be careful not to overbake. I would lean more toward underbaking these.

Tips: Creative Ideas for Delivering Support Gifts

Meal train: A meal train is a thoughtful way to support a friend. This is helpful to support a friend who has experienced a loss, is recovering from a surgery, or has just had a baby. Everyone signs up for a day to bring the person or family a meal. It helps to create a digital sign-up to see who is bringing what so that there is no doubling up on the same food items. When creating this meal train, set the standard by giving an example of what you are providing and including the different elements that each person should bring. It also helps to deliver the food at a specific time so there are no surprises or wasted food left at the door. This consistency is also easier on the friend you're helping. Here are a few classic dinner ideas for a meal train:

- Main dish—a rotisserie chicken, classic chili, or Single-Serve Cheesy Turkey and Kale Stuffed Shells (page 213)
- Side dish—Caesar salad, garlic bread, or mixed veggies
- Dessert—decadent ice cream, brownies, or Classic Chocolate Chip Cookies (page 215)

Something useful: Food, gift baskets, flowers—no matter how you show your support to your friend, deliver the gift with something that can be used again. Take the food in containers that do not need to be returned, and make sure your friend in need knows that too.

Food: If you are delivering food, bring it in a cooler. If you are part of a meal train, share the coolers for drop-offs so that the person receiving the food doesn't have a bunch of coolers by the end of the month. If the food doesn't need to be refrigerated, deliver it in something that adds value, such as delivering a box of pasta and sauce in a colander.

Gift baskets: Baskets full of items I love are my favorite ways to give gifts. However, no one wants to be stuck with a random basket that is useful only at Easter. When giving a gift basket, choose something that is beautiful and useful. Maybe even leave a note in the basket that says how you envision your friend using it. "This basket would be great for _____." I also love thinking outside the basket: a silk pillowcase, a pretty pot, or a bowl make good options.

Flowers: You can't go wrong when it comes to gifting flowers; however, it should be done in a way that requires no effort for the receiver. If you are delivering the flowers yourself, place them in a vase. This may sound simple, but when someone is going through a difficult time, the effort to cut the flowers, find a vase for them, and so on can seem daunting. I also like using items that make surprising vases, like a water pitcher or mason jar.

If the person you are delivering flowers to is dealing with a loss, I find a lot of value in buying them a plant. It will last longer and won't get thrown away in a week.

Label, label, label: If you are delivering food to a friend, make sure all the ingredients are listed and include preparation instructions. If your friend is going through a tough time, this is a great way to tell them you support them in a lighthearted way with an uplifting card. You can also keep it simple and leave a little note saying something like:

- "Dinner is on us."
- "We are here to support you."
- "Wishing you strength and peace."
- "Hoping your treasured memories bring you a little comfort today."

Part Four

Celebrating Sports

I'm going to be honest with you here: my favorite thing about sports isn't who wins or loses. Sorry to all my die-hard sports fans out there, but for me, a big win is when I have a house packed with my favorite people and tables spilling over with delicious apps, snacks, and treats. I may not know who was traded from which team and where, but I know how to put out a spread that will bowl over any sports fan no matter who you root for.

My passion is bringing people together, and sports are a great way for togetherness to happen. When you add a sumptuous feast to the mix, that sense of camaraderie gets a whole lot stronger. Since I was a kid, I've been this way; my favorite part of going to Friday night football games in high school was the community I felt with my friends and the people from my hometown cheering on our team. This feeling followed me when I went to college at Florida State. Florida State has a huge, passionate fan base, and I would have the best time tailgating before the games. As I look back, though, the memories that stay with me aren't the ones of wins or losses but of the laughs shared and bonds strengthened over hot dogs, nachos, and burgers as we had a rollicking good time in the parking lot. I want to share that spirit with you as you have your friends and loved ones over to celebrate big games.

Now that I'm a mom, sports have a whole new meaning. I am in charge of saving the day by providing healthy snacks for my kids' practices and games. I also make sure my kids are powered up for the big competition by ensuring their pregame meals are packed with nutrition. I love it, my recipes are my playbook, and I've got my game face on, so put me in, Coach!

BREAKFAST OF CHAMPIONS

SOCCER MOM SAVES THE DAY

"GO TEAM" TAILGATE

NEIGHBORHOOD FIELD DAY

BREAKFAST OF CHAMPIONS

Feeding a team is a big responsibility. Our kids are out there competing at their best, so let's make sure they are fortified with a breakfast that will have them ready to take on the day. So many weekends are filled with tournaments or road games that require a team breakfast, and sometimes that means taking food to go. It's all about starting the day with a breakfast that makes your team feel like champions—something healthy, hearty, and most of all, delicious.

Set the Scene

Game days are big days! No matter what age your kids are, it helps them to feel supported and know that they have fans rooting for them, even if it's just Mom and Dad. Making sure our little champions see that we are in their corner can be the inspiration they need to get their game faces on.

Make it themed. Soccer, dance, baseball—whatever the sport, add a touch of theme to the breakfast. It can be as simple as tying a piece of tulle ribbon around a muffin for your little ballerina or providing napkins in the baseball team's colors. Showing your colors and cheering on your team is all part of the fun!

Add some inspiration. I am a huge advocate for speaking positively to my kids. I know deep in my heart that positive reinforcement is the best way to bring out the best in the ones we love. If you are preparing a meal for a large group, print out labels with inspirational quotes on them and add them to the breakfast items. If you are providing support for a solo-sports star, as with tennis or dance, an inspirational card slipped into their on-the-go breakfast will go a long way—even if it's just a note on a Post-it!

CANVAS BANNER

Back in my playing days as a kid, and even when I was doing theater in college, I loved having quotes and sayings in places where I could see them as a reminder to stay motivated. No matter what you have going on, you can look at this canvas sign first thing in the morning and get that extra little pep in your step so you're ready for the day! Plus, I love any reason to incorporate puff paint into a craft, and since Tulip's Dimensional Fabric Paints come in a rainbow of colors, you can create an endless number of designs for these fun banners.* This is a craft sure to get the kids, family, and friends involved. Let's go! (photo pages 224 and 229)

MAKES 1 SIGN

Iron

Canvas fabric

Fabric scissors

Ruler

Pen or pencil

Hot-glue gun

Fabric glue, optional

Tulip Brush-On Fabric Paint*

Paintbrushes

Iron-on letters and/or designs

Permanent marker and/or fabric marker

Dowel

Twine or ribbon

Iron the canvas so that it can be cut and measured easily.

Use fabric scissors to cut the canvas to the desired length; 18 x 13 is a good size.

Measure about 5 inches from the bottom up on each side and mark it with a pen or pencil.

Starting at the center of the bottom edge, draw a line from the center to the 5-inch mark on both sides to create the point at the bottom of the banner. Cut on these lines with the fabric scissors.

Use the iron to fold over each side of the banner (except the top) about 1/4 inch so the edges are clean and won't fray. Make sure to fold the corners to create a sharp fold. Use a glue gun or fabric glue to secure each side; the back will have the folded sides.

Flip over the banner and create your design with Tulip Brush-On Fabric Paint, iron-on letters, felt letters, Tulip Dimensional Fabric paint, or permanent or fabric markers, making sure to leave 2 to 3 inches at the top to be folded over.*

Once the design is dry, flip the banner over. Fold the top over the dowel and use hot glue or fabric glue to secure it so the dowel is able to hold the banner.

Attach twine or ribbon to the sides of the dowel and hang.

---

*   Sponsored product; see author's note on page ix.

Tips

- When using iron-on letters, it helps to use a ruler as a baseline when placing them onto the canvas to keep them straight.
- Make the banner from felt instead of canvas. I *love* using felt because it doesn't fray. If you use it for this project, you do not need to fold the sides of the banner over ¼ inch because you don't have to worry about fraying.
- Get the kids involved! Have them think of sayings that inspire them or do their own lettering.
- Customize your banners for your favorite sports teams, and hang a bunch to make adjustable wall decor that can change throughout the seasons.

---

*   Sponsored product; see author's note on page ix.

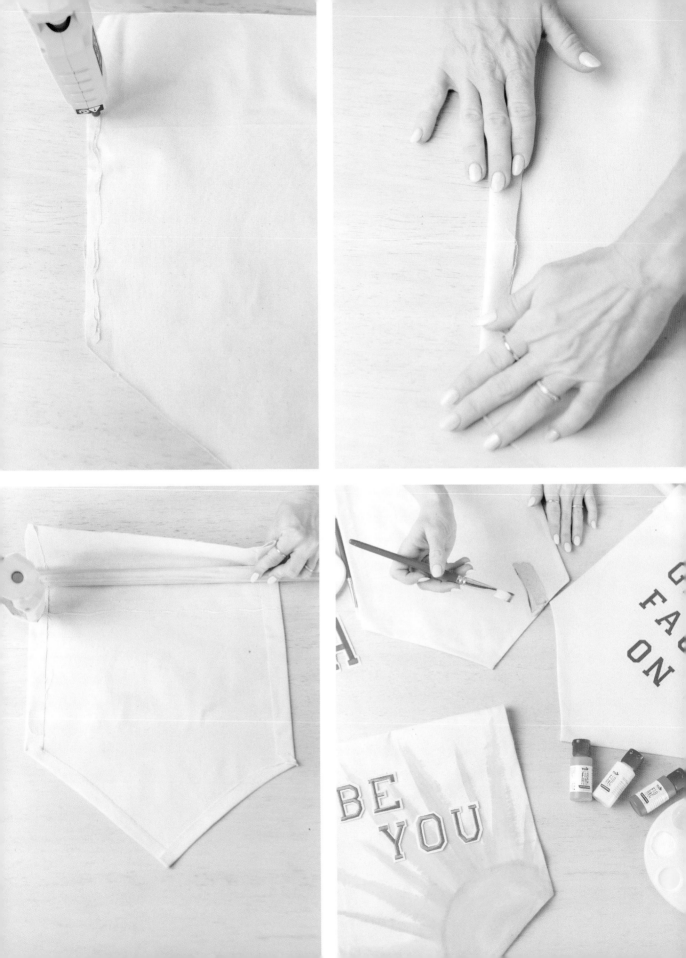

ON-THE-GO PANCAKE MUFFINS

Can a pancake be a muffin? Yes, my friends, it can! This recipe offers the same textures and flavors of a pancake but in muffin form so that it can be taken to go. I wanted to make these a bit heartier and healthier, so I added whole wheat flour and oats. Of course, it's not a pancake without the syrup. Instead of pouring or dipping, the maple syrup is stirred into the batter so that each bite is infused with the lovely maple goodness.

MAKES ABOUT 24 MUFFINS

Nonstick cooking spray
1 batch Champions Brown Sugar Sour Cream Pancake batter (page 106)
1/2 cup maple syrup
1 cup mix-ins, such as chocolate chips, blueberries, etc.

Preheat the oven to 350 degrees. Line a 12-cup muffin pan with liners and spray them with nonstick cooking spray.

Mix up the pancake batter and add the maple syrup. Fold in additional mix-ins.

Fill muffin cups 3/4 full.

Bake for 12 to 15 minutes or until the muffins are puffy and golden and set in the center.

Cool slightly before serving.

Tips

- Use a cookie scoop or measuring cup to scoop the batter into the muffin tins so that it is evenly distributed.
- To keep these warm on the go, place the muffins into an aluminum foil to-go container and cover with foil.
- These pancake muffins can be made ahead of time by baking them, allowing them to cool completely, then placing them in a freezer bag labeled with the date and freezing for up to 3 months. They can go straight from the freezer to the microwave when ready to enjoy.

BREAKFAST SANDWICHES TO FEED A TEAM

Feeding a team can feel like a huge undertaking, but you cannot go wrong with these hearty breakfast sandwiches. The sheet pan eggs are an unexpected addition that will wow your team and capture that "fast food" breakfast sandwich feel.

MAKES 24 SANDWICHES

Cooking spray

2 pounds sausage meat, not in casing

12 large eggs

1/2 cup whole milk

1/2 cup unsalted butter, divided: 1/4 cup at room temperature, 1/4 cup melted

2 (12-roll) packages of Hawaiian sweet rolls

1/4 to 1/2 cup maple syrup, optional

10 ounces shredded cheese, such as a four-cheese blend

Sea salt to taste

Preheat the oven to 350 degrees.

Spray a 9 x 13-inch rimmed baking dish with cooking spray. Spread the sausage evenly in the bottom of the prepared pan.

Spray another 9 x 13-inch rimmed baking dish with cooking spray, line with parchment paper, and spray again. Whisk the eggs in a bowl with the milk and pour into the lined baking dish.

Bake both the sausage and the eggs for 18 to 22 minutes or until the eggs are set and the sausage reaches an internal temperature of 170 degrees.

Remove either the sausage or eggs from their pan so it is available to use for the sliders. Clean the pan, then use a pastry brush or your hands to spread the butter around and evenly coat it.

Slice through the Hawaiian rolls horizontally and place the bottoms of the rolls in the prepared baking dish. Layer the sausage over the rolls and drizzle with maple syrup, if using.

Place the eggs over the sausage and sprinkle the cheese over the eggs. Place the tops of the rolls over the cheese and coat them with the melted butter by using a pastry brush. Add a sprinkle of sea salt over the tops of the buns.

Bake for 10 to 15 minutes or until heated through and the cheese is melted.

Use a knife to follow the lines of the rolls and slice through the layers to form individual sandwiches. Serve hot and enjoy!

Tips

- Make these ahead of time by cooking up the individual layers of sausage and eggs and storing them in the fridge. Then, assemble before cooking.
- Customize the eggs by adding additional ingredients, such as mushrooms or veggies.
- Take these to go by wrapping them individually in aluminum foil.

YOGURT POPS

Popsicles are at the top of the list of my kids' favorite foods. I wanted to find a way to make them healthier so the kids could enjoy them at breakfast time and feel like they are having a treat first thing in the morning. This is a great snack for a team during the hot months as well. They are refreshing and can travel easily in a cooler.

MAKES 10 TO 12
(2-OUNCE) POPSICLES

1 cup berries

2 tablespoons honey

2 cups unsweetened Greek yogurt

1/4 cup whole milk

1 teaspoon freshly grated lemon zest

Popsicle mold

Place the fruit and honey in a blender or processor to roughly break up the fruit.

In a bowl, mix together the yogurt, milk, fruit/honey mixture, and lemon zest.

Evenly distribute the yogurt among the popsicle molds and freeze.

Tips

- Just about any fruit will work. Raspberries and blackberries are my favorite.
- Agave is a great replacement for the honey.
- The amount of sweetener added depends on the sweetness of the fruit. Add as much or as little as desired.
- If you want a smooth appearance instead of a swirled look, put everything in the blender and blend until smooth.
- To remove the popsicles from the molds, loosen the handle of the mold gently and run the mold under warm water, if necessary.

BANANA BREAD

Lots of banana bread recipes call for oil, but although I like how oil makes the bread moist, it doesn't add any flavor. Coconut oil could work, but the mix of bananas and coconut makes me feel like I should be on a tropical vacation. Melted butter is great for flavor, but the bread doesn't come out as moist as I would like. The answer, my friends, is olive oil. Boom, heaven! This is an easy recipe and a good one to make with your kids.

MAKES ONE 9 X 5-INCH LOAF

1 3/4 cup unbleached all-purpose flour

1 cup sugar

1/2 cup brown sugar

1/2 teaspoon salt (I like using kosher)

1 teaspoon ground cinnamon

1 teaspoon baking soda

2 large eggs, room temperature

1 cup mashed ripe bananas
(about 2 to 3 bananas)

1/2 cup olive oil

1/3 cup sour cream, room temperature

2 teaspoons vanilla extract

In a bowl, whisk together the flour, sugar, brown sugar, salt, cinnamon, and baking soda.

In another large bowl, whisk the egg, mashed banana, olive oil, sour cream, and vanilla extract to combine.

Whisk the flour mixture into the banana mixture, stirring until just combined. Be careful not to overmix.

Spray a 9 x 5-inch loaf pan with cooking spray. Pour the batter into the prepared loaf pan.

Bake at 325 degrees for 60 to 90 minutes or until a toothpick comes out clean.

Allow the loaf to cool for about 15 to 20 minutes, and then remove the loaf from the pan to cool on a cooling rack.

Tips

- To make sure the loaf comes out of the pan easily, it helps to line the loaf pan with parchment and spray it with cooking spray.
- This bread freezes beautifully. I like to double the recipe to make two loaves—one to enjoy right away and another to freeze for a rainy day.
- My favorite way to serve these is with a thick layer of peanut butter on a freshly cut slice.

Tips: Breakfast On the Go

Feeding a champion can take a champion. The trick is in the planning! Here are five tips for on-the-go success.

- **Make it ahead of time.** The freezer is your friend when it comes to prepping a team breakfast. That way the food can be heated up first thing in the morning without your having to wake up at the crack of dawn.
- **Make it seasonal.** If your champions are playing summer soccer, they may want food that isn't as heavy and hearty as what a ski team wants in the winter. Customize the recipes to fit the season.
- **Know your audience.** When making food for a team, it's important to know if there are any dietary restrictions or allergies.
- **Travel like a pro.** Keep hot items warm by using thermoses and foil, and use coolers and ice packs to chill colder items like fruit and popsicles.
- **It takes a team to feed a team.** If you are in charge of making breakfast for an entire team, then you know the effort that goes into it. Family members are team members as well. Create a sign-up for each game or tournament where food is needed and allow each family to chip in to make the breakfast of champions.

SOCCER MOM SAVES THE DAY

Sports are great for kids, teaching them resilience, determination, team-building skills, and so much more. And soccer is one of those rite-of-passage sports that most children can't wait to dive into. It also means that early Saturday mornings are game days for the whole family. From team pizza parties to snack breaks, being a soccer mom is hard work; any mom who has cleaned a grass-stained uniform will tell you. Whether the kids are like little bees in a swarm around the ball—just hoping for a chance to kick it—or are kicking playoff-winning goals, they both need the same thing: snacks! As a soccer mom myself, I know that snack time at the end of the game is almost as exciting as the game itself. Win or lose, the snacks can save the day, and that's worth celebrating.

Set the Scene

You know you are officially a soccer mom or soccer parent when you look forward to the games as much as the kids do. The camaraderie is so joyful as the parents cheer over their kids all working toward the same goal. The best way to find success as soccer parents is to work together. Whether it's finding the location of the soccer field, bringing the team sign, or coordinating team apparel, doing basically anything that unites the team and lends a helping hand is supportive and makes you the ultimate soccer mom.

SOCCER SNACK WAGON

Time after time, I saw so many parents dragging bags of food and drinks out to the soccer fields. Necessity is the mother of invention, and I'm a soccer mom with a big necessity. A snack wagon not only helps transport the food to the field but also provides the perfect place for the kids to grab their snacks. When your little athletes see the snack wagon approaching, they are sure to be screaming, "*Goal!*" (photo pages 240–41)

SOCCER BALL HUBCAPS

MAKES 4 HUBCAPS

4 white foam sheets big enough to cover the centers of your wagon wheels

Wagon

Pentagon template (draw or print from online and cut out)

2 to 4 black foam sheets

Pencil

Craft scissors

Hot-glue gun

Butyl tape or Velcro strips

Cut the white foam sheets in circles large enough to cover the centers of the wagon wheels.

Use a pencil and the pentagon template to trace 24 pentagon shapes on the black foam sheets.

Cut out the pentagons using craft scissors.

For one wheel, place one of the pentagons in the center of the white circle. Then, evenly spread out the other pentagons around the wheel. A good way to do this is to place the other pentagons across from the points on the middle one (see photos for a visual). Attach the pentagon shapes with a little hot glue. Cut off the excess pieces of the pentagons so they don't overhang the circle.

Attach the foam sheet to the wagon wheel with butyl tape or Velcro sheets.

Tips

- You may need to use an X-ACTO knife to cut a small hole in the foam where the wheel gets filled with air.
- Glue that's too hot can melt the foam sheet. Either use the glue gun on its "cool" setting or use a very small amount of the glue.
- If you want the soccer wheels to be temporary and easily removed, use a more lightweight tape, such as duct tape or packing tape. Apply the tape on the inside of the wheel so that the tape can't be seen.
- Dress up the wagon by adding some team spirit with a Pennant Garland (page 256). Attach two 1 x 2 pieces of wood to the inside of the wagon with strong Velcro for easy installation and removal.

TEAM SIGN

MAKES 1 SIGN

Ruler

Pencil

Foam core or wood sheet

Cutting mat

X-ACTO knife

Vinyl letters, either premade or customized with a cutting machine, or paint

Velcro strips

Use a ruler to measure out on the wagon what size the sign should be.

Use a pencil to draw the sign to size onto a piece of foam core.

Cut out the sign by placing the foam core onto a cutting mat and use an X-ACTO knife with a fresh blade.

Attach the letters to the sign, or paint if desired.

Attach the sign to the wagon with Velcro strips.

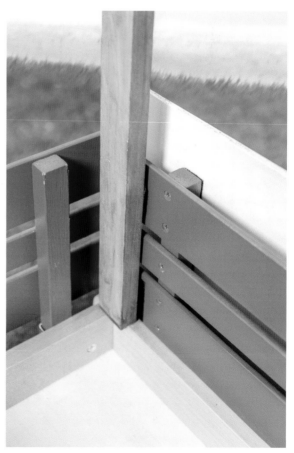

CHERRY, CHOCOLATE, AND COCONUT HOMEMADE GRANOLA BARS

Granola bars are a go-to snack to grab at the store, but once you make them from scratch, you will never go back; I guarantee it. These homemade granola bars are chewy, packed full of flavor, and made without any of the preservatives or additives generally found in popular store-bought granola bars. This recipe is easy to customize by swapping in your favorite flavors.

MAKES ABOUT 12 BARS

3 cups oats (regular or old-fashioned)

1/2 cup unsweetened shredded coconut

1/2 cup chocolate chips (I like using mini)

1/2 cup dried cherries

1/2 teaspoon kosher salt

1/2 teaspoon cinnamon

1/2 cup honey

1/4 cup olive oil

3/4 cup peanut butter

2 large eggs, room temperature

1 teaspoon vanilla extract

Optional add-ins: sunflower seeds, pumpkin seeds, dried fruit, chia seeds

Preheat the oven to 350 degrees.

In a large bowl, combine the oats, coconut, chocolate chips, cherries, salt, and cinnamon.

In a small bowl combine the honey, olive oil, peanut butter, eggs, and vanilla extract.

Pour the honey mixture into the oat mixture and stir until well combined. This will be a stiff mixture.

For easy removal, line a 9 x 9-inch baking dish with parchment paper and spray with cooking spray. Firmly press the mixture into the pan in an even layer.

Bake for 17 to 20 minutes, until the edges start to become golden and the center is set.

Let cool completely before cutting into bars. Wrap each bar in parchment if serving individually.

Tips

- Sunflower seed butter is a perfect replacement to make these nut-free and peanut-free.
- An 8 x 8-inch baking pan can be used instead, but the bars will take about 3 to 5 more minutes to bake, and they'll be a bit thicker and chewier.
- Make sure to allow the granola bars to cool completely before cutting so that they are easier to cut through.
- These bars can be made up to three days in advance and stored at room temperature or in the fridge.

CROSTINI PIZZA TEAM PARTY

Ordering pizzas for after the game is the quick and easy thing to do, but I have a from-scratch solution that is just as quick but even more exciting. I love the idea of getting kids involved as much as I can, so creating a make-your-own-pizza bar is perfect for a team dinner. Take away the stress of dealing with pizza dough and make these on crusty bread. Not only is this a healthier alternative to delivery, but it's also a fun-loving activity to keep your soccer stars entertained.

MAKES 2 PIZZAS

1 loaf ciabatta, baguette, or French bread

1 cup tomato sauce or Homemade Marinara Sauce (page 143)

2 to 3 cups shredded mozzarella cheese

Toppings: pepperoni, mushrooms, bell peppers, pesto, goat cheese, sun-dried tomatoes, Parmesan cheese, bacon, ham, pineapple

Preheat the oven to 400 degrees.

Slice the bread loaf in half lengthwise. Spread sauce onto each half of the bread. Sprinkle each side with cheese and cover with toppings.

Place the bread on a half-sheet baking pan that is lined with aluminum foil. Bake for 15 to 20 minutes or until the cheese is melted and bubbly. For a toasty topping, turn on the broiler for an extra minute.

Slice into 2-inch-wide pizza sticks and serve.

Tip

If the kids are making these themselves, set up a pizza-making station by placing the ingredients into little bowls.

SOCCER BALL COOKIE CAKE

Something magical happens when the flavors and textures of chocolate chip cookies and buttercream are combined. I don't like to play favorites with my desserts, but this combo is definitely at the top of the list. Cookie cakes are great for team celebrations because they are easily customizable and can even be gluten-free if needed.

MAKES ONE 4-LAYER, 8-INCH CAKE

2 batches of Classic Chocolate Chip Cookies dough, divided (page 215)

2 (8-inch) circle baking pans

Parchment paper and pencil

Scissors

Cooking spray

2 batches Buttercream Frosting (page 250)

Offset spatula

Black food coloring

2 piping bags and small circle piping tips

Pentagon template (draw or print from online and cut out; for an 8-inch cake, make a 2-inch pentagon)

1 toothpick or kabob skewer

Preheat the oven to 350 degrees.

Make one batch of the Classic Chocolate Chip Cookies dough.

Place a baking pan over the parchment paper and trace with the pencil. Use the scissors to cut the parchment into a circle that fits inside the baking pan. Spray the uncovered baking pan with cooking spray, then place the parchment in and spray again. Repeat with the second pan.

Split the cookie dough between the prepared baking pans and evenly spread it out with a knife or offset spatula. Bake for 20 to 30 minutes or until the edges become golden and the middle is set. Let the cookies cool completely, then remove them from the pans.

Repeat with another batch of cookie dough to create a 4-layer cake.

Place one of the giant cookies onto the desired platter and top with a thick layer of frosting; repeat with the other three layers.

Spread a thin layer of frosting around the cake so that the cookies can still be seen. My favorite tool for this is an offset spatula.

Place 1/2 cup of frosting into a bowl and add black food coloring to it. Stir until the frosting is evenly colored and nicely pigmented. Prepare a piping bag with a small circle tip (I used a size 1) and fill the bag with the black frosting.

Place the pentagon shape onto the center of the cake and use a toothpick to outline the shape. Repeat around the outside of the circle to resemble the look of a soccer ball (see photos). Outline the pentagons with black frosting, and connect each shape with a line of thin black icing (see photos). Fill in the outlined shapes with the black frosting. (I changed my tip to a wider one, a size 10, for this part.) Use an offset spatula to gently smooth out the filled-in black shapes.

Tips

- Use sugar cookie dough instead of chocolate chip, if desired.
- When piping frosting, make sure to squeeze from the top of the bag, not at the tip.
- It helps to use a rubber band to tie the top of the bag to prevent frosting from coming out the back of the bag.
- This cake can be decorated for any occasion. You could even add edible flowers on the top.
- To see the full layout and visualize the final outcome, use 6 pentagon templates instead of 1.

BUTTERCREAM FROSTING

MAKES 3 CUPS

1 cup (2 sticks) unsalted butter, room temperature

1 pound powdered sugar

2 teaspoons vanilla extract

2 to 4 tablespoons whole milk, room temperature

Using the paddle attachment on a stand mixer, or with a hand mixer and a large bowl, mix the butter to break it up a bit. Slowly add in the powdered sugar with the mixer on low.

Once the sugar and butter start to combine well, turn up the speed on the mixer to medium and add the vanilla extract. Then, pour in 2 tablespoons of the milk.

Scrape down the sides of the bowl to make sure everything gets mixed in and becomes smooth and lighter in texture, about 2 to 3 minutes. If the frosting is too thick, add more milk; if it starts to break up or is not thick enough, add mor powdered sugar.

Use the frosting to decorate cakes, cookies, and cupcakes; it holds its shape well.

Tips: ## DIY Time-Saving Hacks for a Snack-Time Win

- **Wrap food items individually and bring napkins.** Kids' hands are all kinds of dirty when they are playing sports. Wrapped food, like granola bars, helps to prevent their dirty little hands from touching everything you worked so hard to make. I like bringing wet wipes in an attempt to make their hands slightly cleaner before digging in.
- **Bring a cooler.** Make sure it has wheels so that it is easy to tow. This is especially good for those scorching-hot game days.
- **Don't forget the trash bags.** Kids like to open snacks right away and need a place to put the wrappers, juice boxes, and other trash. Having trash bags available is a good way to show kids how to be responsible for the environment and clean up after themselves.
- **Pack extra for siblings and coaches.** Game day is family day on the fields, and team members' siblings love being included. And coaches put so much work into games, so they always appreciate getting a snack.
- **Have a place for the kids to sit and eat.** Depending on the weather, all you need is a big blanket. I like using a waterproof blanket just in case the fields are slightly damp.

"GO TEAM"
TAILGATE

Fall is practically synonymous with tailgating season. There is nothing like getting a crew together to celebrate and enjoy game-day fun! Cheering on your team is such a blast, but the way to elevate your game-day fun is with tons of great food and by showing your team spirit. Since no game day is complete without a little pre-kickoff celebration, this section is all about creating the easiest and chicest tailgate ever. These ideas aren't just for football season; they are perfect for almost any sport.

Set the Scene

Tailgating is all about team spirit and team pride. It doesn't matter if you're decorating your car or your house—showcasing your team's colors is the easiest way to make your space festive and show who you're rooting for. Adding height and texture with decorations like garland or balloons, along with a banner or flag, shows your team pride. You'll turn heads when you hang these banners from your home or your pickup truck! Keep in mind that a little presentation goes a long way. Add some pillows and comfy blankets to transform your folding chairs or outdoor furniture into a plush hangout space. Make sure all your pieces do double duty. Boxes and baskets that you use to transport your food make for the perfect table or stand. And you can never underestimate the power of florals, so add some flowers in your team colors and you're ready for the game.

FELT PENNANT AND GARLAND

Using the right decorations for your tailgate will make you the MVP. I love the old-school look of a classic pennant. It is a simple way to add team spirit and a retro feel to the tailgate. These triangles can also be cut and made into a garland for festive decor. I make these decorations for every Super Bowl, and they are always a major crowd-pleaser. (photo pages 220 and 255)

MAKES 1 PENNANT

Ruler

Pencil

Felt sheets

Fabric scissors

Decorative options: additional felt and fabric glue, iron-on letters, logos

Dowel

Hot-glue gun or industrial-strength glue

Using a ruler and pencil, create the pennant by drawing a triangle on one of the felt sheets.

Cut along the lines on the felt with fabric scissors.

Create wording with the felt sheets by tracing and cutting out letters and attaching them with fabric glue, or using iron-on letters or logos and attaching with an iron as directed.

Use fabric glue to attach additional felt details, such as borders and designs.

Attach the felt to a dowel with hot glue or industrial-strength glue that is safe to use on fabrics.

PENNANT GARLAND

MAKES 1 GARLAND

Ruler

Ribbon or twine

Fabric scissors

Felt sheets

Pencil

Fabric glue

Measure the desired length of the garland and cut the ribbon or twine to size.

Decide on the desired size of the pennants, considering how they will fit on the garland. When used alongside the large Felt Pennant, these look best when they are about half that size so that the large pennant stands out.

Draw the triangles on the felt with a ruler and pencil. Cut out the triangles with fabric scissors. Repeat until there are enough triangles to cover the length of the garland.

Lay out the triangle pennants in a row on a long, flat surface, and place the ribbon or thread along the top of the pieces. Attach the ribbon or thread to the felt with fabric glue. Allow the glue to dry completely; this can take a few hours, depending on the weather.

Tips

- Stiff felt is great for the base of the pennant because it will hold its shape nicely. Stiff felt can also be used for making the Pennant Garland. If you cannot find stiff felt, use regular felt sheets.
- I like using a rotary cutter and cutting mat when cutting larger shapes out of fabric.
- Make the garland at least a day in advance so the glue has time to dry.
- When making the garland, it helps to create one triangle to use as a template for the additional triangles. This will save lots of prep time!
- Fabric glue is the recommended adhesive because it allows the fabric to be washed and is more durable. If this needs to be made in a pinch, hot glue can replace the fabric glue.

ITALIAN SANDWICH

Big sandwiches are an easy way to feed a crowd. That's why this layered sandwich is a go-to for game days. The Roasted Red Pepper Pesto adds an elevated twist on the classic Italian sandwich flavors. This hearty sandwich is sure to win over your tailgate!

MAKES 1 TO 2 SANDWICHES, DEPENDING ON BREAD SIZE

2 (10- to 12-inch) filone rolls (or ciabatta rolls, baguette, or classic hoagie sandwich bread)

4 tablespoons olive oil

1 to 2 teaspoons dried Italian seasoning

1/2 to 1 teaspoon crushed red pepper flakes, optional

2 to 4 tablespoons Roasted Red Pepper Pesto, optional (page 53)

6 slices sharp provolone cheese

3 ounces prosciutto, sliced thin

4 ounces mortadella, sliced thin

3 ounces hot soppressata salami, sliced thin

2 large tomatoes, sliced

1/2 cup thinly sliced red onion

2 to 4 tablespoons peperoncini

Salt and freshly ground black pepper to taste

1 to 2 cups arugula

Cut the rolls in half lengthwise.

Drizzle the inside of each piece with about 1 tablespoon of olive oil, then sprinkle with Italian seasoning and crushed red pepper, if using. Add 2 to 4 tablespoons of the Roasted Red Pepper Pesto to the inside of the bread that will be the bottom slice.

Layer the provolone on top of the pesto. Layer the prosciutto, mortadella, and salami on top of the cheese. Fold the meat over to add height to the sandwich instead of laying the meat flat.

Place the tomatoes, red onions, and peperoncini over the meat. Sprinkle it with salt and pepper.

Top the sandwiches with the arugula. I like to add another drizzle of olive oil over the arugula at this point, but that's optional.

Place the tops of the sandwiches onto the arugula. Insert toothpicks through the sandwich to hold it together. Cut into 3-inch pieces and place on a platter to serve a crowd.

Tips

- ◼ If traveling, pack this sandwich by wrapping it tightly in aluminum foil. Store in a cooler until ready to serve.
- ◼ Change up the meats as needed. Remove the hot soppressata and crushed red pepper flakes if it's too spicy, and use Genoa salami instead.
- ◼ To serve the sandwich hot, wrap it tightly in aluminum foil and warm in the oven at 375 degrees for about 10 minutes or until heated through.

FRIED PICKLES AND DIPS

Growing up in the Midwest, I'd never even heard of fried pickles, but after my first experience tailgating in the South, I wondered how I'd gone my entire life without them. After much research and discussion with my friends who are from the South, I came up with a recipe that I can only hope will do these pickles the justice they deserve.

MAKES 4 TO 6 SERVINGS

Oil for frying (amount will depend on the fryer size)

1 (24-ounce) jar kosher dill pickles cut into circles (aka "chips")

1 1/2 cups all-purpose flour

1/2 cup cornmeal

1/2 teaspoons seasoned salt (I like Lawry's)

1/2 cup buttermilk

1 large egg

Additional salt for topping

DIPPING SAUCE OPTIONS

Honey Mustard (page 14)

Herby Ranch (page 14)

Homemade Marinara Sauce (page 143)

Pour enough oil into a Dutch oven with a candy thermometer attached to reach a depth of 2 inches. If using a fryer, fill according to the specific brand directions. Heat the oil to 360 to 375 degrees.

Drain the pickles, then place them on a baking sheet or plate lined with a paper towel to help them dry. This will help the batter adhere to the pickles.

In a large bowl, mix together the flour, cornmeal, and seasoning salt, and set aside.

In a medium bowl, whisk together the buttermilk and egg.

Dip a small batch of pickles in the buttermilk mixture until they are well coated, then dip them into the flour mixture. Shake off the excess flour.

Carefully place the coated pickles in the hot oil. Flip the pickles with a spider strainer or tongs after a minute or two to cook the other side. Remove the pickles from the oil when they are golden.

Place the fried pickles on either a paper towel or a cooling rack placed over a lined baking sheet to prevent them from getting soggy. Add an additional sprinkle of salt while the pickles are still hot. Allow the pickles to cool for just a few minutes before serving.

Tips

- Use an oil with a high smoking point. I like using sunflower oil.
- Work in batches for the best outcome. Frying too many pickles at once can cause the oil temperature to lower, which creates a soggy snack.
- If the mixture gets clumpy in the dipping process, just add a couple of tablespoons of flour to help fluff it up again.

ROOT FOR THE HOME TEAM "CRACKER JACKS"

Okay, okay, I know "Cracker Jacks" are a baseball thing, but I can have them any day of the week and be happy. This recipe is perfectly sweet, salty, and crunchy, and a great snack to eat while rooting for your team.

MAKES APPROXIMATELY 10 CUPS

Cooking spray

10 cups popped popcorn (unsalted and unflavored)

1 cup butter

1/2 cup light brown sugar

1/2 cup sugar

1/2 teaspoon baking soda

1/2 teaspoon salt, preferably kosher

1 cup roasted peanuts

Line a half-sheet baking pan with parchment paper and spray it with a little cooking spray.

Place the popcorn in a large bowl.

Place the butter, brown sugar, and sugar in a saucepan over medium-high heat. Stirring continuously, bring the butter and sugar mixture to a boil. Once it reaches a steady boil, let it cook for 4 minutes without stirring.

Stir in the baking soda and salt; the mixture will become foamy. Continue to stir for another 30 seconds.

Once the caramel mixture is well combined, stir in the peanuts. Pour the caramel over the popcorn. Using a spatula, stir well to coat the popcorn evenly.

Pour the mixture onto the prepared baking sheet and spread out into an even layer.

Allow the popcorn to cool, stirring every few minutes with your hands until completely cooled.

Tips

- Boiling the sugar mixture can be a bit of an art. I have definitely undercooked and overcooked this recipe many times. An undercooked mixture will be chewy, and an overcooked one will be burnt. The trick is to start the timer when you see a steady boil and then, right at the 4-minute mark, add the baking soda.
- The caramel mixture is very hot, so it's not one for the kids to help prepare.
- Continue to stir as the caramel cools on the popcorn; this helps to evenly distribute the caramel.

Tips: Tailgate Success

Frozen water bottles: It's always a good idea to have water on hand, so why not get more bang for your buck? Freeze the water bottles ahead of time, and when game day rolls around, just pop them in the cooler instead of ice.

Pop-up trash bins: Keep your tailgate location clean by providing your fellow tailgaters with a place for trash. I also like to have an additional pop-up bin for items that can be recycled, like bottles and boxes.

Folding chairs: These may seem obvious, but they tend to be forgotten. I like folding chairs that have a back on them. They are much comfier and easier for kids to sit on.

Extra blankets: Blankets always come in handy, no matter the temperature. They can be a place to sit if your tailgate is on a field, and long game days can often turn into cool nights. Blankets are especially important for chilly tailgating days; inevitably, someone won't dress for the weather and will need additional layers.

A tent for hot days: I've tailgated in Florida, so trust me when I say this one is lifesaving. A little shade goes a long way when the heat is in the upper nineties. A portable fan can save the day as well.

A portable grill: If you are a dedicated tailgater, a portable grill is a great investment because it helps cut down on prep time and allows for cooking while tailgating.

Yard games: Ladder ball, cornhole, ring toss, or even just throwing a ball back and forth can make tailgating more enjoyable. Giving everyone something to do while hanging out is a great way to get conversations and laughs started.

Snack food: Even if you are making all the delicious food I share in this section, having extra snack food around is a good way to keep bellies full and to stretch the homemade food further. Fruit, veggies, chips and salsa, or other easy snacks that don't require preparation will save you time. Have a few of these on hand, especially if you have any picky eaters at your tailgate.

NEIGHBORHOOD FIELD DAY

The end of the school year calls for a giant field day for the whole school. When I was a kid, field day felt like freedom: a worry-free day filled with competition, friends, silly games, and, of course, food! Field days aren't just for school, though. I am a huge believer in the power of cultivating community, and hosting a gathering for some friendly competition is a great way to get to know your neighbors and create new, lasting relationships, traditions, and memories.

Set the Scene

A field day is all about enjoying the outdoors. Spread out the games so that it's obvious which supplies and props go with which games. Making signs for each game is also a good idea. Establish a home base that serves as a place for people to find snacks and seating, and set up a craft table for the little ones who aren't into the games. Having a structure to the day is helpful too. Start with an opening ceremony where each team is recognized and writes their name on the scoreboard. Then, create a schedule that allows for each team to play each game. FInally, end the day with a closing ceremony and some treats.

---

*   Sponsored product; see author's note on page ix.

TROPHIES

Since we are celebrating friendly competition, every kid should be able to walk away with a prize. I like to provide kids with craft supplies so they can create their own trophies. Keep in mind the ages of the kids involved and provide supplies that are easy to use for each age group. I love letting kids use puff paint for their creations. The three-dimensional effect from Tulip Dimensional Paint makes the trophies feel almost like the real thing.* Your little athletes will be beaming with pride to show off their creations.

MAKES 1 TROPHY

Butcher paper to cover the work surface

Painter's tape

1 small bucket

1 small block of wood that the bucket fits on

Hot-glue gun

School glue

Nontoxic paint in various colors

Paper plates or artist palettes

Variety of paintbrushes

Tulip Dimensional Paint in various colors*

Foam stickers

Pom-poms

Cover the work surface with butcher paper and secure it with painter's tape.

Place the supplies on the table so the kids can pick which items they want and have creative freedom.

Attach the bucket to the top of the wood block; either an adult can hot-glue it or kids can secure it with school glue.

Allow the kids to decorate the trophies however they like.

Tips

- Kids can use school glue to attach the bucket to the block, but it takes much longer to dry, so consider doing this step ahead of time.
- Provide cups of water and paper towels so the kids can rinse and dry their paintbrushes as needed.
- Create a designated spot for the trophies to dry so families can grab them on their way out.

---

* Sponsored product; see author's note on page ix.

CHICKEN KABOBS

These chicken kabobs are easy to prep the day before and grill up hot and fresh for the outdoor celebration. These make for great, and healthy, leftovers—if there are any left!

MAKES 5 TO 6 KABOBS

1/4 cup olive oil, plus more for cooking

1/2 cup buttermilk

1 tablespoon dried Italian seasoning

1/4 cup chopped parsley

2 cloves garlic, minced

The zest and juice of 1 lemon, plus more for topping

1/2 teaspoon kosher salt, plus more to taste

1/4 teaspoon freshly ground black pepper

2 large or 3 small boneless, skinless chicken breasts, cut into approximately 1-inch cubes

In a medium bowl add the olive oil, buttermilk, Italian seasoning, parsley, garlic, lemon zest and juice, salt, and pepper. Whisk until fully combined. Add the chicken to the bowl and stir to coat the chicken evenly. Cover with plastic wrap and place in the fridge for one hour or overnight.

For outdoor grilling, heat the grill until hot and oil the grill to prepare it.

Arrange the chicken pieces on skewers, metal or wooden. Grill for 3 to 4 minutes on each side or until the chicken is no longer pink in the middle.

Sprinkle with a little more salt to taste and a squeeze of fresh lemon juice. I like my chicken lemony, so I add a lot.

Serve with a salad, over rice, or with a favorite dressing for dipping. I like using my Herby Ranch (page 14).

Tips

- Do not marinate for more than 24 hours as it can break down the chicken too much.
- Soak wooden skewers in water for an hour before using. Soaking can prevent them from catching on fire when on the grill.
- For indoor cooking, place a cast-iron grill pan over medium-high heat and add a little olive oil to prepare it for cooking the kabobs.

HONEY AND BASIL FRUIT SALAD

If you're working up a sweat out in the sun, having fruit is a must! Fruit salad is a go-to whenever we are getting together with families; everyone loves it. The additions of fresh lime juice (to balance out the sweetness), honey (for some floral notes), and basil (for an earthy, herbaceous note) create a balanced salad that feels elevated enough for the adults but will also be loved by the kids.

MAKES 4 TO 6 SERVINGS

4 large ripe yellow peaches, sliced

1 cup raspberries

1 cup blueberries

1/2 cup pomegranate seeds, optional

6 large basil leaves, cut into ribbons or torn into pieces

1 to 2 tablespoons honey

1 lime, divided

Place the peaches, raspberries, blueberries, and pomegranate seeds (if using) onto a platter and top with the basil.

Drizzle the fruit with honey, adding more or less depending on the sweetness of the fruit.

Cut the lime in half and squeeze one half over the fruit. Taste the fruit salad and squeeze the second half of the lime over the salad, if needed.

Tips

■ Use whatever fruit is in season and looks fresh!

■ Agave is a great alternative to honey.

■ Adding basil is optional, but the herbaceous touch elevates the entire salad.

CAPRESE PASTA SALAD

Caprese salad is a beautiful blend of tomatoes, basil, and mozzarella. What's not to like? This recipe takes that classic combination to a whole new level. I use my favorite Lemony Basil Pesto because it adds a nice nutty and tangy flavor, and I turn the salad into a pasta dish that can be served hot or cold.

MAKES 4 TO 6 SERVINGS

1 pound pasta

Salt for salting water, plus more to taste to season pasta

1/2 to 1 cup Lemony Basil Pesto (page 51)

Juice from 1 lemon, divided

1 pint cherry tomatoes

8 ounces mozzarella cheese

Pepper to taste

1/4 cup torn fresh basil leaves

Cook the pasta in a large pot of salted water so it is al dente. Reserve about 1 cup of the pasta water. Strain the pasta, then pour it back into the pot.

Stir in 1/2 cup of the Lemony Basil Pesto and the juice of half of the lemon. Add a small splash of the pasta water to help loosen the pesto and create a sauce.

Cut the tomatoes and mozzarella into about 1/2-inch pieces and add them to the pasta. Mix everything together.

Taste the pasta and add more pesto, lemon, salt and pepper as desired. Add more reserved pasta water, if needed.

Top with fresh basil.

Tips

- I like using ciliegine, which are small balls of mozzarella, in this recipe.
- You can add any protein you like to this pasta salad.
- If serving cold, taste the pasta salad beforehand as it may need additional seasonings.

TORCH CUPCAKES

End the day of friendly competition on a sweet note. The "flame" is created with candy-coating chocolate; it's easy to work with, and when the colors swirl together, it looks like fire. This dessert definitely has a "wow" factor! (photo page 264)

MAKES ABOUT 24 CUPCAKES

Vanilla Cupcakes batter (page 276)
24 ice cream cones with flat bottoms
Candy coating chocolate (aka candy melts) in red, orange, and yellow
Buttercream Frosting (page 250)

Preheat the oven to 325 degrees.

Cover a 9 x 13-inch baking pan tightly with aluminum foil. Cut 12 evenly spaced holes into the foil and place one cone in each hole so that 12 fit in one pan.

Prepare the cupcake batter. Fill the cones with batter about 2/3 of the way up.

Bake for about 20 to 25 minutes or until the middle is set.

Allow the cupcakes to cool completely while preparing the frosting and "flames."

To create the flames:
Melt the chocolate in three separate bowls in a double boiler or microwave.

Scoop the melted red chocolate onto the wax paper and spread around with the spatula. Top it with the melted orange chocolate and spread it around with the spatula. Place a scoop of the yellow chocolate into the orange chocolate and spread that around to create a fire look.

Place the chocolate spread in the fridge to harden. Once it is hardened, use your hands to break it into pieces to look like fire.

Top the cupcakes with frosting. Add a piece of the chocolate flame.

Tips

- The chocolate flames can be made in advance and kept at room temperature.
- Don't use too much frosting or the cupcakes will become too top-heavy once the flames are added.

VANILLA CUPCAKES

Cooking spray

3 cups all-purpose flour

1 teaspoon baking powder

1/2 teaspoon baking soda

1/2 teaspoon salt

1 cup unsalted butter, room temperature

2 cups sugar

5 large eggs, room temperature

1 cup buttermilk, room temperature

1/3 cup mild-flavor oil, such as sunflower oil

2 teaspoons vanilla extract

Preheat the oven to 325 degrees. Spray a 12-cup muffin pan with cooking spray or add cupcake liners.

In a bowl, whisk together the flour, baking powder, baking soda, and salt. Set aside.

In a stand mixer with a paddle attachment, beat the butter and sugar together on medium-high speed until light and fluffy, about 2 minutes. With the mixer on low, stir in the eggs one at a time until each one is combined, being sure to scrape down the sides of the bowl.

Stir the buttermilk, oil, and vanilla extract together in a small bowl.

With the mixer on low, add in 1/2 of the dry ingredients and mix until just combined. With the mixer still running on low, add in the milk mixture. Stir in the rest of the flour mixture and mix until just combined, being careful not to overmix.

Scoop the batter into the muffin pan. Bake for 25 to 35 minutes or until a toothpick inserted in the center comes out clean.

Tips: Plan a Winning Field Day

Stick to the classics. Neighborhood field days are all about the classic games, such as ring toss, corn hole, lawn darts, and potato sack races, to name a few.

Encourage team spirit. Have each family dress in the same colors or pick a theme.

Keep score, but make it fun. Create a scoreboard on a chalkboard or dry-erase board and put it where everyone can see. Add points for things like "best victory dance" or "most creative trophy" to keep everyone on their toes.

Switch up the hosts. Each family can take a turn hosting the backyard competition. To choose the next host, draw a name out of a hat or go in alphabetical order.

Make it a tradition. Add a little more incentive to win by having an actual trophy made; each year, the name of the winning family can be added. This way you can remember all the winners over the years. Neighborhood bragging rights are on the line!

Part Five

Celebrating Seasons

When I was growing up in the Midwest, I loved everything about living in a place that experienced the seasons to the fullest! I always embraced the exhilarating change from season to season; it felt so magical and transformational. I remember looking forward to the first sign of the season changing and the hope that always came as the first leaf turned colors in fall, the first snowflake appeared in winter, the first robin chirped in spring, and the first warm summer breeze filled the air. Seasonal crafts and recipes help me enjoy and soak up each season as much as possible and celebrate the rebirth and renewal that change can bring. Each change of season feels like an invitation to experience something new. Join me in commemorating each season in all its glory.

SNOW-DAY PLAY

SPRING GARDENS

SUMMER CAMP CLASSICS

I can't say enough good things about summer camp! I so looked forward to seeing my camp friends, making friendship bracelets, trying new things like canoeing, and being introduced to being independent as a growing, young girl. Summer camp is a great experience for kids to break out of their shells and see what they are capable of. It's where lasting memories are made and formative experiences are forged. Summer camp is a place for kids to be free from technology, connect with nature, and have the time of their lives outdoors with their friends.

Set the Scene

To create the summer camp experience in your own home, start with lighting. Lighting a bonfire, setting out candles, or hanging a few strings of lights outside will spark that camp vibe. Whenever I want that summer camp feeling, I know I can always transport myself there with food. Grilling over an open flame is a surefire way to bring that camp experience home. Adding a little char to your feast can make all the difference, and trust me, the scent will evoke that camp feeling right away. Don't forget to dine alfresco; summer nights should be spent outdoors, under the stars, so grab your plates and let the moon light your way!

CAMP SIGN

You've got to love the no-frills, rustic, outdoorsy feel of summer camp. At the camp I went to growing up, hand-painted signs directed you to the hiking trail or to the lake grounds for swimming and boating. I thought, why not transport some of the camp vibes to my home? (photo page 282)

MAKES 1 SIGN

Acrylic paint or wood stain in desired colors

Paintbrushes

3 to 5 wooden arrow signs

Paint pen, optional

Vinyl lettering, optional

Sandpaper, optional

2- to 3-foot flat wood stake

Wood glue

Paint or stain the wooden signs in the colors desired and allow them to dry completely.

Write on the signs with a paint pen or paint, or add vinyl lettering.

Once the paint has dried, use the sandpaper to buff away some of the paint to make the sign look weathered, if desired.

Attach the wood signs onto the wood stake with wood glue and allow to dry completely.

Once the glue is dry, stick the wood stake in the ground.

Tips

- This sign can be made as large or as small as desired. Adjust the size of your wood stake accordingly.
- Let the kids design and paint the wood signs themselves.
- Using a cutting machine to create the vinyl lettering is helpful if creating different fonts isn't in your wheelhouse.
- To make a base so the sign will stand on its own, screw a 1 x 4 piece of wood into a wood round.

GRILLED CORN SALAD

Yum, fresh corn in the summer—you just can't beat it. By the end of summer in Michigan, the corn tastes so sweet; it's almost like eating candy. As a kid, I couldn't wait to grab an ear off the grill and slather it with butter and salt. I'm taking that classic flavor and adding it to a salad that is so good even the kids will eat it.

MAKES 4 SERVINGS

4 ears fresh corn, husks and silks removed

1 to 2 tablespoons avocado oil (or another high-heat oil)

1 teaspoon salt

1 red bell pepper, diced

1 pint cherry tomatoes, cut into quarters

1/2 cup thinly sliced red onion

1/2 cup julienned basil leaves

1 tablespoon chives

1 to 2 avocados, cut into roughly 1/2-inch pieces

1/2 cup crumbled feta

2 tablespoons olive oil

2 to 4 tablespoons fresh lime juice to taste

1 teaspoon honey

1/2 teaspoon salt, preferably kosher, plus more to taste

1/4 teaspoon freshly ground black pepper, plus more to taste

Heat a grill over high heat.

Drizzle each ear of corn with approximately 1 teaspoon of avocado oil, then rub the oil into the kernels. Sprinkle with the salt.

Place the corn directly on the grates of the grill. Grill, turning every 3 to 4 minutes to cook all parts of the corn, until charred and tender, about 15 minutes. Remove the corn from the grill and set aside until cool enough to handle.

Cut the kernels from the cobs and place into a large bowl. Add the bell pepper, cherry tomatoes, onions, basil, chives, avocado, and feta.

In a separate small bowl, whisk together the olive oil, lime juice, honey, salt, and pepper until well combined. Pour the mixture over the salad and gently toss to combine. Taste for seasoning and add additional salt, pepper, or lime juice if needed.

This salad can be served warm right away or kept in the fridge and served cold.

Tips

- If you are making this recipe for kids, leave out any strong flavors they may not like, such as onions.
- Cotija cheese and goat cheese are good replacements for the feta cheese in this recipe, but feta is my favorite for this. I try to find "goat's milk" feta or a Greek feta because the flavor tends to be creamier.

GRILLED TOMATO TOAST

My grandpa grew the ripest, juiciest, most flavorful tomatoes. He took such pride in raising his tomatoes from little seeds to plump, delicious fruit. He became a victim of his own success because he grew so many tomatoes that he would end up giving them away by the bushel! He didn't mind, though, because he knew they made many people happy.

My favorite way to eat fresh tomatoes is on grilled bread. The char on the bread adds a great crunch and smoky flavor to the bright tomatoes, and a kiss of garlic on the bread adds a lovely bite that balances everything out. Every time I have a bite, I'm reminded of my dear grandpa and the joy he gave to so many.

MAKES 8 TO 10 SERVINGS

4 tablespoons olive oil, plus more for topping

8 to 10 slices hearty country bread

1 garlic clove, cut in half

6 to 8 medium-large heirloom tomatoes cut into slices

1/2 cup fresh basil leaves

1/4 teaspoon crushed red pepper flakes, optional

Sea salt to taste

Freshly ground black pepper to taste

1 lemon, cut in half

Drizzle the olive oil on both sides of the bread slices. Place the slices on a hot grill and cook long enough to achieve grill marks on both sides.

While the bread is still warm but cool enough to touch, scrape the garlic half onto one side of the bread to leave a slight kiss of flavor.

Top the bread with the tomato slices and sprinkle with the basil leaves, crushed red pepper (if using), sea salt, and pepper. Add a squeeze of fresh lemon juice to taste.

Tips

- Make sure the bread is hearty so that it can stand up to the juicy tomato topping.
- Smaller tomatoes, such as cherry, work for this, but I like using the larger ones because I find they stay on the bread more easily.
- Adding the crushed red pepper flakes may be more for the adults, but if the kids are up for the spice, then go for it.
- Balsamic vinegar is a good replacement for the lemon juice to add a touch of sweetness.

WATERMELON LAVENDER LEMONADE

Watermelon is a dessert staple at almost every summer camp. Eating slice after slice, filling our cheeks with the rinds to make silly faces, and seeing how many seeds we could stick to our faces were just some of the antics we would get up to at camp. When I think back to those times, I still can't help but laugh. I let that memory inspire this recipe. I've added watermelon to the classic summer drink, lemonade. I've added lavender as well because there are gorgeous lavender fields in Northern Michigan, and the scent of lavender perfumes the air. This drink is a blend of three flavors that take me back to my summers in Michigan.

MAKES ABOUT 8 CUPS

1 cup sugar

1 cup water

2 tablespoons dried lavender

1 cup freshly squeezed lemon juice (approximately 5 to 6 large lemons, depending on size)

4 cups of cold water

4 cups seedless watermelon, cubed

Lavender sprigs for extra decoration, optional

Lemon slices for decoration, optional

Place the sugar and water into a pan and stir together over medium heat until the sugar dissolves. Whisk the lavender into the pan and stir together.

Once the mixture starts to lightly boil, turn down the heat and simmer the mixture together for about 10 minutes. Simmer for a few minutes less for a lighter lavender flavor. Allow it to cool completely.

In a blender, combine the lemon juice, cold water, and cubed watermelon. Blend until smooth.

Add as much of the lavender simple syrup as desired to the mixture, then blend to combine. I recommend starting with half the amount of the lavender syrup and adding more if needed. To make the beverage more lemony, add more lemon juice.

Store the lemonade in the fridge until ready to use. Add ice to individual glasses and serve!

Tips

- The amount of lavender simple syrup needed will vary based on how sweet the watermelon is and how sweet you like the drink.
- To make this a cocktail, simply add vodka. Start with a shot and go from there.
- Add some lavender sprigs and lemon slices to make these drinks extra fancy.

BANANA BOATS

At summer camp we usually bunked in our cabins, but at least one night we'd camp out under the stars and cook our food over the bonfire. We'd make s'mores, of course, but my favorite was when we made banana boats. If you've never made a banana boat, then get ready for delicious, messy fun. It's basically a s'more, but in a banana!

MAKES 1 BANANA BOAT

1 banana

5 to 7 mini marshmallows

1 tablespoon chocolate chips

1 tablespoon peanut butter or butterscotch chips, optional

1 graham cracker

Cut a slit down the center of the unpeeled banana, but not all the way through.

Scoop out a little bit of the banana to make room for the filling.

Add in the marshmallows, chocolate chips, and peanut butter or butterscotch chips (if using).

Break the graham cracker into pieces and add to the banana. Press the banana together to close the slit as much as possible.

Tightly wrap the banana with a piece of aluminum foil. Place the wrapped banana over a bonfire on a grill for about 10 minutes, flipping halfway through, or until the inside is melted and gooey. To cook in an oven instead, bake at 375 degrees for about 10 to 15 minutes or until the inside is nice and gooey.

Tips: Backyard Campout Success

- It isn't camping without a tent! Whether it's a real tent or a makeshift tent, it will add the magical element of relaxing under the stars.
- Don't forget the blankets and pillows. Load up your space with cozy elements to bring your outdoor camping experience to the next level.
- Put up a giant screen in the backyard to show movies—fun for kids and adults alike.

AUTUMN
COLORS

Oh my, do I love the fall. The crispness in the air, leaves changing color, the smell of bonfires, pumpkin patches dotting the roadways—everywhere you look, you feel like you are living in an artist's landscape. Fall makes me think of new beginnings as many of us start back to school, come back from our summer vacations, and renew the spirit of taking on new adventures. I feel inspired by the beauty of the season. It's a lovely reminder that both change and growth are beautiful and should be celebrated. So let's harvest some positivity and growth as we let the season of fall inspire our creativity and passion.

Set the Scene

I love bringing that outdoorsy fall feeling into my home during the autumn months. Adding earth-tone elements and touches of warm colors to my interior decor brings a warmth that will cozy up any space. I like to fill a vase or two with dried flowers or beautiful mums to create a palette of color that will beautify my home. Putting out fall-inspired candles will bring an amber glow and an aromatic pleasantness that soothes and delights. And, of course, baking up a batch of Fall Leaf Sugar Cookies (page 308) will take your home from zero to fall faster than you can say "pile of leaves"!

FLANNEL DRINK SLEEVES AND COASTERS

When I can create a DIY with supplies I have lying around the house, I feel like a crafting superhero. This is one such craft, but before I go and fashion myself a cape, take a look at what you can do with items I'm sure you have tucked away in your home. This craft turns that flannel button-down shirt you have in the back of your closet into festive and functional fall decor. The drink sleeves and flannel coasters are so cute you'll be racing to whip up your favorite warm fall drinks. (photo page 298)

DRINK SLEEVES

MAKES 2 SLEEVES

Fabric scissors
1 long-sleeve flannel shirt with cuffs
Fray Check, optional
Elastic hair ties

Cut the cuff of the sleeve off the shirt just above the seams. Trim away any excess fabric from the seam. Seal the cut edge with Fray Check if needed. Allow the glue to dry.

If the drink sleeve is too small for your cup, feed a hair tie through the buttonhole, then feed one loop of the hair tie into the other. Pull taut. The flexibility of the elastic hair band allows any size cuff to fit any size cup.

Secure the drink sleeve onto your cup using the button.

COASTERS

MAKES 4 TO 6 COASTERS

Fabric scissors

1 long-sleeve flannel shirt

4 to 6 (4 x 4) cork coasters

Fabric glue or hot-glue gun

Felt

Lay your square coaster onto extra flannel fabric from the shirt used to make the drink sleeves. Cut the flannel with about a 1-inch seam allowance around the coaster.

Fold the fabric onto the back of the coaster. Secure with fabric glue or hot glue.

Cut a piece of felt slightly smaller than your coaster and glue to the bottom with fabric glue or hot glue. Allow the glue to dry completely.

Tips

- The felt at the bottom makes the bottom of the coaster even and also creates a flat, soft base to go onto a table.
- Fabric glue allows for cleaning the fabric and also allows the fabric to get wet without it affecting the adhesive. If using hot glue, there is a risk that the adhesive won't hold as well if exposed to moisture.

PUMPKIN PIZZA

You got me: I'm one of those "pumpkin-obsessed" people. I add pumpkin into everything I can in the fall, and pizza is no exception. I like to make this recipe with my homemade pizza dough, but it can be made with a premade dough of your choice as well.

MAKES 2 PIZZAS

2 tablespoons olive oil

1 shallot, finely chopped

1 teaspoon salt

2 garlic cloves, minced

1 teaspoon finely chopped fresh sage

1 teaspoon finely chopped fresh oregano

1/4 teaspoon ground nutmeg

1 cup pumpkin puree

Pizza Dough for 2 pizzas (page 302)

Cornmeal as needed

1/4 cup Gruyère cheese

1/4 cup Parmesan

Pumpkin Seed Pesto (page 53)

1/2 teaspoon crushed red pepper flakes, optional

4 ounces burrata cheese

2 heaping cups arugula

Olive oil for topping

Sea salt to taste

Freshly cracked pepper to taste

Tools recommended: pizza stone, pizza peel, pizza cutter

Heat the olive oil in a medium skillet over medium heat. Add the shallot and salt and cook, stirring frequently, until the shallot has softened. Add the garlic, sage, and oregano. Cook until fragrant, being careful not to brown the garlic (about 30 seconds). Stir in the nutmeg.

Add the pumpkin puree and stir to combine the flavors together. Lower the heat to a simmer and cook for about 4 to 6 minutes, stirring often.

Place a pizza stone in the oven and preheat the oven to 500 degrees (yes, 500 degrees).

Stretch the dough with the back of your hand and knuckles, or manipulate it like a steering wheel. Everyone likes to do this differently. If you are feeling ambitious, toss it in the air!

Place the stretched dough onto a pizza peel that has been covered with cornmeal.

Spread the pumpkin mixture evenly between the two pizzas. Top with the Gruyère and Parmesan.

Use the pizza peel to carefully (and sometimes quickly) place the pizza directly onto the stone. Bake for about 10 to 15 minutes or until golden and bubbly.

Use the pizza peel to take the pizza out of the oven and place it on a large cutting board.

Add drizzles of the Pumpkin Seed Pesto around the pizzas and sprinkle on red pepper flakes if desired. Break up the burrata and place it around the pizzas. Top with arugula and a drizzle of olive oil, and season with sea salt and pepper.

Cut the pieces with a pizza cutter and eat it while it's nice and hot.

Tips

- Be sure to use pumpkin puree and not pumpkin pie filling.
- If you have issues with the pizza dough sticking to the pizza peel, place the dough onto a piece of parchment before adding on all the toppings. This helps transfer it easily in and out of the oven. The downside, in my experience, is that the crust doesn't get as crispy as it does when it is put directly onto the stone.
- To add another savory element, top this pizza with crumbled sausage or bacon.

PIZZA DOUGH

MAKES 4 MEDIUM PIZZAS

2 1/2 cups warm water (around 110 to 115 degrees)

1/4 cup sugar

1 packet of instant yeast (around 2 1/4 teaspoons)

6 cups 00 flour, plus more for rolling out

2 teaspoons salt

1/4 cup olive oil, plus more for coating

Pour the warm water into the bowl of a stand mixer. If it is a cool day, prep the bowl ahead of time by running it under some warm water and then drying it with a clean towel. This way, the bowl won't lower the temperature of the water.

Stir in the sugar and yeast.

Allow the mixture to sit for about 10 minutes, until it becomes frothy. If this doesn't happen, it means your yeast is not good and you need to start over with new yeast. Once it starts to get frothy, you can smell the delicious "bread" smell that yeast creates.

In a separate large bowl, combine the flour and salt together with a whisk.

With the mixer on low using a dough hook attachment, stir in the olive oil.

Mix in the flour by adding about 1/2 cup at a time to slowly incorporate the flour. Turn the speed to medium and continue mixing until the dough can be pulled away from the sides of the mixing bowl with a spatula. If it is too wet, you can add a little more flour, but this is a sticky dough, so do not add too much. The dough will stick to your fingers when you try to touch it.

Add some olive oil to a large bowl so that the entire inside of the bowl is lightly covered in the oil. Use a spatula or pastry scraper to scrape the dough into the oiled bowl. Turn the dough to coat it in oil.

Cover the bowl with a tea towel, or something similar, and let the dough rise at room temperature until it has doubled, about 1 to 2 hours. I like to put the dough in the oven (with the oven turned off, of course) to avoid any drafts or changes in temperature, especially if it's cold out.

Once the dough has risen, turn it out onto a well-floured work surface. Sprinkle the dough with additional flour, and cut it into four equal pieces. Use your hands to cover each piece with flour and pull the dough around to the bottom, stretching it to create a smooth ball.

Cover again with a tea towel until you are ready to use it. If you are using it within 30 to 60 minutes, then you can leave it out, but if you are making this ahead of time, you can place it in the fridge.

When you are ready to make the pizzas, bring the dough back to room temperature. This can take about an hour.

Tip:

- Pizza dough freezes beautifully. Store in a freezer-safe container in the freezer for 3 to 4 months. Allow it to come to room temperature before using.

FALL PASTA E FAGIOLI WITH SAGE PESTO

Butternut squash is another one of those perfect fall flavors, so it only makes sense to add it to one of my favorite Italian soups. I add a touch of a sage drizzle to the top of the soup to accentuate all the fall flavors. This warm and cozy soup is a bowl full of heaven on a crisp fall day.

MAKES 6 TO 8 SERVINGS

6 ounces pancetta, chopped

2 tablespoons olive oil

2 large carrots, finely chopped

1 fennel bulb, finely chopped

1 onion, finely chopped

1 teaspoon salt

2 garlic cloves, minced

1 (15-ounce) can crushed tomatoes

1 (15-ounce) can cannellini beans, drained and rinsed

5 cups vegetable stock

2 cups water

2- to 3-inch rind of Parmesan, optional

1 cup ditalini, or similar-shape pasta like tubettini or elbow

2 cups Roasted Butternut Squash (page 305)

Sage Pesto (page 306)

Freshly ground black pepper for serving, optional

Add the pancetta to a large pot or Dutch oven over medium heat. Cook, stirring frequently, until the meat starts to brown. Remove the meat using a slotted spoon and place onto a plate lined with a paper towel until needed.

In the same pot, add the olive oil, carrots, fennel, onions, and salt. Turn the heat to medium-high and cook until the vegetables start to soften.

Stir in the garlic and let cook until fragrant, about 30 seconds. Stir in the tomatoes and bring to a simmer. Simmer for 5 to 7 minutes, stirring every so often.

Add the beans, then pour in the stock and 2 cups of water. Add the cheese rind, if using. Bring the soup to a boil, then reduce the heat and simmer for 5 minutes.

Add the pasta and adjust the heat to maintain a low simmer. Cook, stirring occasionally, until the pasta is al dente, around 8 to 10 minutes.

Stir in the Roasted Butternut Squash during the last few minutes of cooking.

Ladle the soup into bowls, drizzle with the Sage Pesto, and sprinkle with the crispy pancetta and black pepper, if desired.

ROASTED BUTTERNUT SQUASH

MAKES APPROXIMATELY 2 TO 3 CUPS

1 butternut squash, about 2 to 2 1/2 pounds

2 to 3 tablespoons olive oil

1/2 teaspoon salt, preferably kosher

Preheat the oven to 375 degrees.

Peel the butternut squash and cut into 1/2-inch cubes. Place on a baking sheet lined with aluminum foil and toss with the olive oil and salt.

Bake until softened, about 30 minutes.

SAGE PESTO

MAKES ABOUT 3/4 CUP

3 to 4 tablespoons fresh sage

1 cup fresh basil

1/2 cup freshly grated Parmesan cheese

1 garlic clove

8 tablespoons olive oil, or enough to make the pesto able to drizzle off a spoon

2 teaspoons fresh lemon juice

Salt and pepper to taste

Make the pesto by placing the sage, basil, grated Parmesan, and garlic into a food processor, and slowly add the olive oil until you achieve the right consistency; the pesto should drizzle off a spoon. Stir in lemon juice, and salt and pepper to taste.

Tips

- Pecorino is a great alternative to Parmesan for finishing the soup.
- Replace the pesto drizzle with freshly grated Parmesan, a drizzle of olive oil, and torn fresh basil and sage. I love the pesto, but if you do not have time to make it, this is a good alternative.
- You can replace the Parmesan rind with 1/4 cup of freshly grated Parmesan. I would add it to the soup when adding the Roasted Butternut Squash.

SLOW-COOKER PUMPKIN SPICE LATTES WITH FALL LEAF SUGAR COOKIES

I need my coffee no matter the season, but once that temperature starts to dip, you better believe that the first cup of joe in the morning is a full-on necessity. In this recipe, I combine my obsession with all things pumpkin and pumpkin spice with my favorite beverage. And because I can't leave well enough alone, I'm sharing my recipe for a cookie that has all the colors of the fall. Add them to the warm pumpkin spice latte to make a pretty fall-themed mug that's filled with the colors and flavors of the season. (photo page 294)

MAKES ABOUT 14 CUPS

3 cups half-and-half

3 cups whole milk

6 cups strong coffee

1 1/2 cups pumpkin puree

2 tablespoons vanilla extract

1 cup sweetened condensed milk

1/2 cup maple syrup

2 teaspoons Pumpkin Pie Spice

Freshly whipped cream, optional

Cinnamon stick, optional

In a slow cooker, whisk together the half-and-half, whole milk, coffee, pumpkin puree, vanilla extract, condensed milk, maple syrup, and Pumpkin Pie Spice until fully combined. Cook on high for 1 to 2 hours, stirring every 20 to 30 minutes.

Flavors can be adjusted as necessary: use more coffee for a stronger drink, add more syrup for a sweeter drink, and so on.

To serve, pour into mugs and top with freshly whipped cream and cinnamon sticks.

PUMPKIN PIE SPICE

MAKES APPROXIMATELY 4 1/2 TABLESPOONS

3 tablespoons ground cinnamon

2 1/2 teaspoons ground ginger

1 teaspoon ground nutmeg

1 teaspoon ground cloves

1 teaspoon ground allspice

1/4 teaspoon cardamom, optional but highly recommended

In a medium bowl, whisk together the cinnamon, ginger, nutmeg, cloves, allspice, and cardamom (if using) until combined. Use fresh spices for the best results.

Transfer the spice mixture to a sealed container and store at room temperature.

Tips

- I like using one part whole milk and one part half-and-half for the perfect level of creaminess.
- I used maple syrup to sweeten this recipe, but you can also use brown sugar.
- Once the latte is done cooking for a couple of hours, leave it on the "warm" setting to prevent the milk from overcooking.

FALL LEAF SUGAR COOKIES

5 1/2 cups all-purpose flour

2 teaspoons baking powder

1/2 teaspoon salt

1 cup unsalted butter, room temperature

1 1/4 cups sugar

1 cup coconut oil, measured at room
temperature, melted, and cooled

2 large eggs, room temperature

1 teaspoon vanilla extract

Food coloring in fall colors, such as
red, orange, green, and yellow

Sanding sugar for topping, optional

In a large bowl, whisk together flour, baking powder, and salt. Set aside.

In a stand mixer cream together the butter and sugar until light, fluffy, and pale in color.

Slowly add in the cooled coconut oil and mix well. Stir in the eggs one at a time and mix until combined. Mix in the vanilla extract.

Slowly add in the flour mixture and stir until completely mixed in. Be careful not to overmix.

Divide dough into 4 sections to make 4 different colors, and add a few drops of food coloring into each dough section. Mix the dough and coloring together with a spatula until it is well combined and the dough is the desired color. Be careful not to overmix.

Break up the different doughs into smaller pieces and spread them around a surface covered with wax paper and sprinkled with flour so that they are evenly distributed. Use your hands to bring the dough together slightly. Sprinkle with a little bit of flour. Cover with wax paper. Use a rolling pin over the wax paper to roll the dough out into a flat disk; if you would like the colors to be more swirled, remove the wax paper and fold the dough a bit, and then reroll.

Roll the dough to about 1/4 inch thick. Place in the fridge and chill for 20 to 30 minutes.

Remove from the fridge and use leaf cookie cutters to cut out shapes. Optional: cut a small slit into the cookie about the thickness, or slightly larger, of the rim to the mugs that will be used for the pumpkin spice lattes.

Place the shapes onto a baking sheet lined with parchment paper. Sprinkle sanding sugar over top of the cookies, if desired.

Bake at 350 degrees for about 10 minutes or until slightly golden on the edges. Allow to cool completely. Once the cookies have cooled, place them onto the rim of the mug. (photo page 294)

Tips: **Festive Fall Sightseeing**

One of my favorite things to do in the fall is drive around to look at the tapestry of leaves changing color. Here are a few ways to make it extra special.

Bring a festive drink. You could bring Slow-Cooker Pumpkin Spice Lattes (page 307) or hot apple cider.

Place the drinks in a mug. And don't forget to pair them with a lovely DIY Flannel Drink Sleeve (page 297).

Pack up fall food. Put the Fall Pasta e Fagioli (page 305) in a thermos to keep it warm. Pack the Fall Leaf Sugar Cookies (page 308) in a container that is easily accessible, as those can be eaten during the drive.

Get cozy. Pack a few blankets, wear a cozy sweater, and stop for a breath of fresh air. The best part about sightseeing is being able to stop and to enjoy the moment.

SNOW-DAY PLAY

I vividly remember, when I was growing up in Michigan, running downstairs to watch the local news in hopes that there was enough snow for the schools to call for a snow day. There is something so special about staying home from school to play outside in a big, white blanket of snow and then coming inside for warm food and hot chocolate. I also remember my mom saying that she hoped the snow day was only one day—and now, as a parent, I understand why. It can be a lot of work for parents to entertain the kids on these cold and snowy days. I am bringing you solutions via DIY that are fun whether you are in a snowstorm or you live somewhere warm and are longing for a winter-white day.

Set the Scene

As we settle into winter, I like to create cozy feelings of warmth in my home. I'll repurpose greenery from the holidays and thoughtfully place it in vases around the house. I'll add lots of winter white with blankets, candles, and table linens. To balance the winter whites, I use wood rounds and birchwood branches to fill the spaces where the holiday decorations were located. This will add notes of warmth to your at-home winter wonderland.

SNOWY PUFF PAINT

Keeping kids entertained during a snow day can seem daunting. They can only play in the snow for so long before they want to cozy up inside. And sometimes it is just too darn cold out! So let's bring in some of that snowy fun without all the mess. This paint is best for ages four and up; use your discretion.

MAKES ABOUT 2 CUPS OF PUFF PAINT, BUT THE MIXTURE WILL EXPAND

1 cup school glue
1 cup foamy shaving cream
Medium bowl
Spatulas
Nontoxic paint
Paintbrushes
Cardstock or thick paper
Plastic squeeze bottles, optional
Additional decorative elements: googly eyes, glitter, sticks, foam sheets

In a bowl, use a spatula to mix together equal parts glue and shaving cream until they are well combined. Add paint to the mixture if desired.

Use the paintbrushes to apply the paint to paper, or fill a plastic squeeze bottle with the paint and squeeze the paint out.

Add additional decor if desired.

Tips

- Use shaving cream that doesn't have a strong smell. Believe me: if you don't, your kids will smell like it for the rest of the day.
- Make sure to use the "foamy" shaving cream, not gel.
- The best glue for this is nontoxic school glue.
- For safety, I also recommend nontoxic paint.

HOMEMADE POPCORN BALLS

My mom and I always made popcorn balls during Christmastime. We'd bring them to holiday parties, give them as gifts, or put them out at local events. Making and eating them always serves as such a fond reminder of special times in my life. The crunch and flavor of these light and lovely, sweet confections are a perfect winter treat. Plus, they look like a snowball, so that adds a nice festive touch to any snow-day celebration.

MAKES 6 TO 10 BALLS,
DEPENDING ON DESIRED SIZE

4 tablespoons unsalted butter

1/4 cup firmly packed brown sugar

10 ounces marshmallows

1 teaspoon vanilla extract

12 heaping cups popcorn

Cooking spray or additional room-temperature butter for coating hands

Sea salt for topping

Prepare a baking sheet by lining it with wax paper.

In a large, heavy pot, melt the butter over medium to low heat. Stir in the brown sugar and marshmallows. Continue stirring until the mixture is almost completely melted. Remove the pot from the heat.

Stir in the vanilla extract. Stir in the popcorn and mix until well coated. Allow the mixture to cool enough so that it can be handled.

Coat your hands with the cooking spray or butter. Scoop out the desired size of the popcorn ball and use your hands to shape the mixture into a ball. Place it onto the wax paper. Sprinkle with sea salt.

Tips

- Regular sugar cannot be substituted for the brown sugar. The molasses in the brown sugar makes these rich and caramelly.
- When I want to be extra fancy I like to drizzle the popcorn balls with melted chocolate and top them with sprinkles.

TURKEY CHILI

There is no better way to warm up after a day of making snow angels than with a warm bowl of chili. This recipe is a take on my mom's special recipe for turkey chili. After meeting a number of chefs who are passionate about chili, I added minor tweaks and techniques to take this classic to the next level.

MAKES 14 TO 16 CUPS

2 tablespoons unsalted butter

1 tablespoon olive oil

1/2 cup finely chopped carrots

1 red onion, finely chopped

2 large celery stalks, finely chopped

1 teaspoon kosher salt, divided, and more to taste

2 tablespoons chili powder

2 tablespoons garlic powder

1 tablespoon cumin

1 tablespoon dried thyme

1 teaspoon dried oregano

1/2 teaspoon cayenne pepper

1/2 cup red wine, preferably a full bodied

2 pounds organic ground turkey

2 cups vegetable broth

2 (15-ounce) cans diced tomatoes

2 (15-ounce) cans tomato sauce

1 (15-ounce) can kidney beans, drained and rinsed

1 cup frozen corn, defrosted

Pepper to taste

1/2 cup freshly chopped parsley

In a large, heavy saucepan or Dutch oven, melt the butter and oil over medium heat.

Add the carrots, onions, and celery. Sprinkle with half the salt. Sauté until softened, about 5 minutes.

In a small bowl, combine the chili powder, garlic powder, cumin, thyme, oregano, and cayenne. Add the spice mixture to the softened onions and celery. Stir and cook until aromatic, about a minute.

Add the wine and cook it for about a minute to cook off the alcohol.

Stir in the turkey, breaking it up into smaller pieces, and cook the meat through.

Add the broth, tomatoes, and tomato sauce. Mix in the beans and corn.

Bring mixture just to a boil, then reduce the heat to medium-low and simmer for about 30 to 45 minutes. If the mixture is too thick, add some water, up to 1 cup.

Season with salt, pepper, and any additional spices as needed. Stir in the parsley and serve hot.

Tips

- A trick to knowing when the alcohol has cooked out of the wine is to smell it. If it smells acidic, let it cook a little longer. If it smells smooth, move on to the next step.
- I recommend using frozen or fresh corn for this recipe. Canned corn tends to be too salty and soft for my taste.
- Top the chili with shredded cheese and a little sour cream for a finishing touch that will wow the crowd. Or if you want to be extra fancy, top the chili with Cheese Sauce (page 12).

HOMEMADE HOT CHOCOLATE AND HOMEMADE MARSHMALLOWS

When I'm making a batch of hot chocolate, I like to add special elements to create the perfect cup. I make up a batch of my favorite chocolate sauce that can go on just about anything (like on a spoon, and then directly into your mouth, but I digress) and mix it with some warm milk. If you really want to separate your hot chocolate from the pack, top it with Homemade Marshmallows. (photo page 310)

HOT CHOCOLATE

MAKES 1 SERVING

8 ounces whole milk
2 tablespoons Fudgy Brown Sugar Chocolate Sauce (page 319)
Homemade Marshmallows for topping (page 320)

Warm the milk in a small saucepan until bubbles just start to form, being careful not to scald the milk.

Stir in the chocolate sauce and use a whisk to combine. Add more chocolate if desired.

Pour the hot chocolate into a mug and top with Homemade Marshmallows.

FUDGY BROWN SUGAR CHOCOLATE SAUCE

MAKES 1 3/4 CUPS SAUCE

1/3 cup cocoa powder, preferably Dutch processed
3/4 cup firmly packed brown sugar
1/4 teaspoon salt
1 cup whole milk
1/2 cup dark chocolate chips
1 cinnamon stick, optional
1 tablespoon espresso or strong coffee
1 teaspoon vanilla extract

Combine the cocoa, brown sugar, and salt in a small mixing bowl with a whisk.

Pour the milk into a small saucepan. Add the cocoa mixture to the milk and whisk together.

Continue to whisk over medium heat and add in the dark chocolate chips. Add the cinnamon stick, if using.

Continue to whisk and bring the mixture to just under a boil. Reduce the heat to low and simmer for about 5 to 8 minutes, until everything is incorporated. Remove the pan from the heat and whisk in the coffee and vanilla extract.

Use immediately, or let cool completely and store in the refrigerator in a sealed container.

Tips

- There is absolutely no reason to skimp when it comes to this recipe, so use whole milk.
- For a sweeter hot chocolate, semisweet chocolate can be used in place of the dark chocolate.
- This recipe can be made with dairy-free chocolate chips and any dairy-free milk of choice.

HOMEMADE MARSHMALLOWS

MAKES ABOUT 32 LARGE
MARSHMALLOWS

3 tablespoons unflavored gelatin

1/2 cup room-temperature water

2 cups honey

1/4 teaspoon salt

1 vanilla bean and seeds or
2 teaspoons of vanilla extract

Powdered sugar for topping and cutting

Sprinkle the gelatin over the water in the same large bowl you will use for mixing. Let sit for 5 minutes so that the gelatin is absorbed by the water.

Spray a 9 x 13-inch baking pan with cooking spray.

In a medium saucepan, whisk together the honey and salt over medium heat.

Turn the heat to medium-high and bring the mixture to 240 degrees, monitoring the temperature using a candy thermometer and whisking every so often.

When the mixture has reached 240 degrees, slowly add the honey mixture to the gelatin mixture on medium-low speed. Once all the honey mixture is added, turn the mixture to high and beat for about 10 minutes. The mixture should be light and fluffy. It's fun to watch this happen!

While the mixture is starting to fluff up, add the vanilla bean and the seeds (or vanilla extract). Pour the mixture into the prepared baking pan and let set at room temperature, overnight, uncovered.

When the marshmallows are set, remove them from the pan. Sprinkle a cutting board with powdered sugar and use a knife to cut the marshmallows.

Tips

- The marshmallows are best to cut the day after they are made. If they are hard to cut, add more powdered sugar to the top.
- This recipe makes a lot, so I freeze what I don't use and pull them out when I need to make a quick dessert!

Tips: Make a Snow Day Fun

When you are a kid, snow days are pretty much the most magical and memorable thing in the world. Having a chance to get bundled up and play in the snow on a school day? Yes, please! When I was growing up, my mom would always create a fun craft or game for us to play as a family while we were stuck inside. Since we live in LA now, my boys don't get to experience snow days unless we're visiting family or traveling. That's why I wanted to share a few crafts and activities to help make your snow day (real or make-believe) a success! These activities are perfect for kids on a snow day—or any day!—to spark creativity.

Get cozy. Pull out your comfiest outfit and fluffiest blankets to embrace a day of being at home. Make a fun fort or cozy space to play in all day.

Pop outside and breathe the air in. Really breathe it in. If you live in an area with snow, build a snowman, have a snowball fight, try to catch a snowflake on your tongue. Do all of the things you would normally do as a kid, and you will have more fun than you expect.

Go old-school with candles and games. Before you turn on your favorite snow-day movie, get some laughs and friendly competition with a board game or card game. Setting the scene with white unscented candles will make your home feel even more warm and comfy.

SPRING

GARDENS

I jump for joy when it's time to sport pastels and the easygoing, breezy fabrics that capture the spirit of spring. My love for this season goes beyond flowy fashion. Spring is such a joyful season because we get to welcome warm weather. The flowers bloom, and there is an overall feeling of lightness and spontaneity in the air. Plus, in California, we finally get to shed our winter coats because it's seventy degrees outside. I have to laugh: in the Midwest, my parents and neighbors were out washing their cars and wearing shorts as soon as the temperatures hit fifty degrees; in Los Angeles, fifty degrees is still winter!

No matter where you live, you can welcome spring with some light and cheerful decor, recipes, and more.

---

* Sponsored product; see author's note on page ix.

Set the Scene

When I think of spring, I think of eclectic and cheerful beauty. A lovely linen tablecloth topped with woven place mats makes a perfect foundation for a spring table. Curate a beautiful tablescape with various plates, teacups, and china from around the house or that you've found at a secondhand shop. A spring party calls for light pastels and, of course, lots of flowers. Potted plants and wicker baskets full of flowers placed around the table create an elegant atmosphere for your springtime event.

SPRING RESIN TRAY

Epoxy resin is like magic! When the liquid resin is combined with a liquid hardener, it creates a chemical reaction that will become solid and clear. It can be colored, poured, and molded in various ways, and objects can be suspended in the hardened resin. For our spring celebration, let's create a tray that has soft colors and dried flowers.

MAKES 1 TRAY

Silicone tray mold or tray with sides
Hot glue
Disposable gloves
Face mask
Popsicle sticks
Epoxy resin kit (resin and coordinating hardener)
Mixing cups
Glitter, mica powder, or paint in desired colors
Additional decorative materials, such as metallic resin flakes or dried flowers
Heat gun or hair dryer
Drill
Handles

If using a tray with sides, seal the inside of the tray with hot glue so that any cracks are closed; otherwise the resin will seep through.

Work on a covered surface while wearing gloves and a mask. Using a popsicle stick, mix the resin and hardener together in a mixing cup according to the instructions. (See photo page 328.)

Add the glitter, mica powder, or a touch of paint into the mixture. Continue to mix until completely blended. (See photo page 328.)

To create the marbled look, use two different colors plus some clear resin.

Freely pour the colored resin into the mold in an abstract pattern. Move the mold around to spread the resin. (See photo page 329.)

Before you pour the clear resin into the mold, you can add metallic resin flakes and/or flowers to it. (See photo page 329.)

Pour the clear resin into the mold, then move the mold around to blend the resin a little. Just blur the lines a bit—don't blend it so much it gets muddy.

To pop any bubbles on the surface, gently blow warm air on the resin with a heat gun or hair dryer on a low setting.

Allow to cure for 24 hours.

Add another layer of clear resin over the top to create a smooth top to the tray. Allow it to cure for another 24 hours.

Drill a hole to fit the size of the handles and screw set being used. Screw the handle on. (Skip this step if using a premade tray.)

Tip

■ Always work on a covered surface in a well-ventilated area (preferably outside) and wear gloves and a mask.

* Sponsored product; see author's note on page ix.

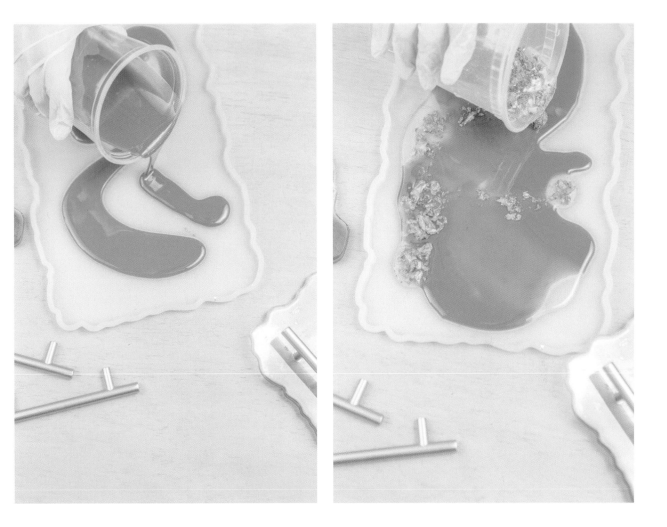

RAINBOW RADISH SALAD

Radishes are one of the most underrated vegetables. I happen to be a big fan. The bright colors, earthy flavor, and crunchy texture make for a perfect springtime salad. This recipe looks like it belongs in a fancy restaurant, but it's easy, effortless, and worthy of any celebration.

MAKES 4 SERVINGS

5 to 7 radishes, enough to have about 2 cups of thinly sliced radishes

1 cup arugula

2 tablespoons toasted pine nuts

2 ounces ricotta salata or feta cheese

Lemony Salad Dressing (page 75)

Salt and pepper to taste

Clean and dry the radishes to be sure all dirt is removed.

Use a mandoline to thinly slice the radishes.

Lay out the arugula onto a platter. Spread the radishes over the arugula. Sprinkle the pine nuts over the radishes.

Shave or sprinkle the ricotta salata over the top. Drizzle the Lemony Salad Dressing over the salad to taste. Add salt and pepper as needed.

Tips

- I recommend using two or three types of radishes. My favorites are watermelon radishes, red radishes, and French breakfast radishes.
- Feta is a good replacement for the ricotta salata. It has a nice briny, salty flavor that works well in this dish.
- A mandoline is not expensive and makes for a great tool in the kitchen. This recipe is a great excuse to get one. If you don't have one, carefully slice the radishes with a sharp knife, but these little guys like to roll around, so do this with caution.
- If desired, replace the pine nuts with nuts of your choice.

SPRING VEGETABLE PASTA WITH ROASTED SALMON

This pasta is light and comforting. Its bright lemon flavor is a wonderful base for the spring veggies to shine. The pop of sweetness from sweet peas is lovely next to the rich and buttery salmon. These flavors work together to create a spring pasta that is crave worthy all year long but is especially perfect on an alfresco evening shared with friends sipping La Gioiosa Prosecco Rosé.* I can't think of a more refreshing way to end a warm spring day!

SPRING VEGETABLE PASTA

MAKES 4 SERVINGS

1 teaspoon kosher salt, plus more for seasoning the water

1 pound spaghetti, linguine, or bucatini

2 tablespoons butter

1 tablespoon olive oil

1 cup thinly sliced leeks, rinsed and dried well to remove dirt

1 cup peas, fresh or frozen

2 garlic cloves, minced

1 tablespoon lemon zest, divided

1/2 cup lemon juice, divided

3/4 cup freshly grated Parmesan cheese, plus more for topping

1/4 cup fresh, torn basil leaves, plus more for topping

Roasted Salmon (page 334)

1/2 teaspoon freshly ground black pepper

Bring a large pot of water to a boil and add enough salt to flavor the water.

Add the pasta and cook until al dente, about 8 to 10 minutes. Reserve 1/4 cup of pasta water in a cup to use later.

Meanwhile, in a large skillet over medium heat, add the butter and olive oil. When the butter is melted, add the leeks and cook for a minute or two until the leeks start to soften. Stir in the peas, garlic, and half of the lemon zest. Cook until the garlic becomes fragrant.

Add half of the lemon juice. Transfer the pasta directly from the cooking water to the large skillet. Pour the Parmesan over the pasta and then toss to combine everything together.

Add the rest of the lemon zest and lemon juice to taste. I like a lot of lemon, so I add it all.

Add the pasta water, about 1 tablespoon at time.

Toss the basil into the pasta. Season with pepper.

Use your hands to break the salmon into large pieces and add it onto the pasta. This can be done in individual servings or in one large serving when feeding a crowd.

Add additional basil and cheese to serve.

---

*   Sponsored product; see author's note on page ix.

ROASTED SALMON

2 tablespoons olive oil, divided

2 (8-ounce) salmon fillets

1/2 teaspoon salt

1 lemon, cut in half

Preheat the oven to 425 degrees.

Drizzle 1 tablespoon of the olive oil in an 8 x 8-inch baking dish. Place the salmon in the baking dish, and sprinkle the salt evenly between the two pieces.

Drizzle the other tablespoon of olive oil over the salmon and squeeze the juice of half of a lemon over the salmon.

Bake the salmon for 15 minutes or until you achieve the desired doneness. Remove the salmon from the oven and squeeze the second half of the lemon over the salmon. Set aside until ready to add to the pasta.

Tips

- Additional spring vegetables, such as peas, can be added to the pasta for even more springtime flavor.
- I add the lemon juice and zest in stages because there is a big difference in cooked lemon flavor and fresh lemon flavor. I cook half the amount of zest and juice to add some richness and depth, then add the rest to finish with a nice, bright pop of acidity.
- One large salmon fillet could be used in this recipe instead of the individual fillets.

MERINGUE WITH BLACKBERRY CURD AND SUGARED FLOWERS

Meringues are one of the most charming desserts on earth. They can be a bit high maintenance, but when you get it right, they are heavenly little pillows of sugar and air. This recipe will help you achieve a crunchy, chewy, delicious outer layer while also creating that marshmallow-like inside treat. Whether you are a seasoned pro or simply looking to impress your friends and family, this recipe fits the bill. (photo page 336)

MAKES ABOUT 12 MERINGUES

6 large egg whites, room temperature

1/8 teaspoon salt

2 cups baker's sugar

1 teaspoon white wine vinegar

1 teaspoon cornstarch

1 teaspoon vanilla extract

Sugared Flowers (page 337)

Blackberry Curd (page 337)

Fresh whipped cream, optional

Preheat the oven to 250 degrees. Line a baking sheet with parchment paper.

Whisk the egg whites with the salt on medium-high speed in a stand mixer or with a hand mixer until soft peaks form. Gradually add the sugar, beating until stiff peaks form and the sugar has dissolved. It's ready when you rub the mixture between two fingers and no longer feel any sugar granules.

Beat in the vinegar, cornstarch, and vanilla extract. Mix until well combined.

Transfer the mixture to a large piping bag fitted with a large plain tip, and pipe evenly spaced mounds (roughly 2 inches in diameter and 2 inches high) onto the parchment. You can also use 2 spoons to scoop out the mixture.

With the back of a spoon, create a hollow in each mound that will be filled once the meringue is baked.

Bake until the meringue easily lifts off the parchment, about 1 hour and 10 minutes. Turn off heat; let the meringue stand in the oven for about 1 hour with the oven door cracked open.

Once the meringue cools, spoon a dollop each of the curd and the fresh whipped cream over the top, and garnish with sugared flowers.

Tips

- Lemon juice or white vinegar can be used in place of the white wine vinegar.
- Baker's sugar, aka "extra fine sugar" or "superfine sugar," is recommended because it dissolves easily into the egg whites and creates a better meringue overall.
- Make sure the sugar is dissolved when whisking. If the sugar doesn't completely dissolve, it will become runny instead of hardening when baked.
- Change up the flavor of the curd to make this meringue throughout the year.
- Start with very clean tools. Meringue is touchy and won't turn out right if it comes in contact with oils. Before I start, I clean my mixing bowl and whisk with vinegar.

SUGARED FLOWERS

MAKES 12 TO 24 FLOWERS

1 egg white

1 teaspoon water

1/2 cup superfine sugar, plus
more if needed

12 to 24 edible flowers,
depending on size

Pastry brush or paint brush
dedicated to food items

Whisk the egg white and water together in a bowl.

Use the pastry brush or a paintbrush to carefully paint the egg wash onto the flowers while holding them with your fingertips or kitchen tweezers.

Sprinkle the flowers with the sugar and place on a cooling rack. I like to place the cooling rack on a baking sheet lined with parchment paper so that I can move it easily, and it helps with cleanup. These flowers could be placed directly onto parchment, but they may become soggy at the bottom. Using the cooling rack allows them to harden on all sides.

Allow the flowers to harden for several hours or even overnight. Hardening times can vary based on weather. Be sure to check them and gently move them every hour or so to prevent them from sticking.

BLACKBERRY CURD

MAKES ABOUT 1 1/2 CUPS

Makes about 1 1/2 cups

12 ounces blackberries

3/4 cup water

3/4 cup sugar

4 large egg yolks, room temperature

1 large (whole) egg, room temperature

4 tablespoons cold, unsalted
butter, cut into small cubes

Combine the blackberries and water in a small saucepan over medium heat. Cook until the liquid bubbles while using a spatula to smash and break up the berries. Once the berries have released their juices (about 8 to 10 minutes), remove them from the heat.

Press the blackberries through a strainer into another bowl. Be sure to scrape all of the juice on the underside of the strainer into the bowl as well. Pour the juice back into the saucepan and set aside for a moment.

Whisk the egg yolks and egg together in a small bowl until combined. While whisking, pour in the sugar and whisk until lighter in color.

Whisk a small amount of the blackberry juice into the egg mixture to temper the eggs.

Add the egg mixture to the blackberry juice in the saucepan, and continue whisking until well incorporated.

Place over medium heat, whisking constantly, until the mixture thickens and coats the back of a wooden spoon, about 8 to 10 minutes.

Remove the pan from the heat and stir in the butter, one tablespoon at a time.

Strain again, into a bowl, to remove any lumps. Cover the surface of the bowl with plastic wrap and chill in the refrigerator for at least 1 hour, or pour into glass jars and allow to cool, then refrigerate.

This curd is thinner than a traditional curd, which makes it easy to pour over the meringue.

Tips: Spring Cleaning

Spring is all about rebirth and new beginnings. I like to celebrate by cleaning out the house. Here are some easy ways to get started.

Start with the closet. It's so satisfying to get rid of clothes that no longer suit me and my life. When my mom helped my sister and me clean our closets each spring, she would tell us to ask ourselves, *How do I feel about myself when I wear this?* If the item of clothing didn't make us feel good or add value, it got tossed in the "donate" pile. It's a small but highly effective and empowering way to start spring cleaning.

Label, but make it pretty. I love to decant my baking ingredients by placing them in pretty jars and adding labels. It keeps everything fresher and looks nicer than a crumpled-up bag sitting in the pantry.

Get the kids involved. I talk to so many parents who say they go through toys and toss them without telling the kids. Now, I am far from a parenting expert, but I think it's important for my little ones to see it takes work to organize the house. It also opens the door to a conversation about why they should donate their items to those less fortunate.

Get rid of the toxic cleaners. Spring is a good time to breathe freshness into your home. As much as I dislike housework, I look forward to it much more when my cleaning supplies are fresh and make my house smell clean while also being safe for my family and the environment.

ACKNOWLEDGMENTS

Creating this book was something I dreamed about my entire life. As a little girl, I would read my mom's cookbooks and imagine what it would be like to test recipes and take pretty photos to inspire other people. It is my firm belief that creativity equals happiness, and my goal with this book is to inspire everyone to get creative. A huge thank-you to the Harper Horizon team for giving me creative freedom and trusting me to make a book that married my two favorite things: crafts and food.

Thank you to everyone who was able to be a part of this wonderful project:

- Eryn Kalavsky, literary agent
- Alison Coen, commissioning editor
- Jenney Korasick, brand editor
- Collective Media, project editor
- Bree McCool, branding and lifestyle photographer
- Becca Kmieciak, photography assistant
- Hope Burns, prop stylist

- Rolando Rangel, prop builder
- Leslie Grow, photographer
- Jaclyn Kershek, prop stylist
- Laura Kinsey Dolph, food stylist
- Food assistants:
  - Max Rappaport
  - Sophia Green
  - Guthrie King

I also want to say a big thank-you to the special people who were able to be in the photos:
Jebby Terry and Jackson Davis, for being such good friends to my boys and good sports for the photos.

Orly Shani and Morgan Presson Kasulis, for being the greatest friends on the planet.

Alison Coen and Jenney Korasick, for believing in me, making me laugh all the time, and being there through the ups and downs.

My husband, Brett Davis, and our two boys, Grant and JJ Davis. These three are everything to me.

Last, but not least, my parents, Anthony and JoEllen Provenzano. I thank God every day that I was given the best parents I could have asked for. It's their unwavering encouragement that allows me to believe that anything is possible.

INDEX

About the Author

Maria Provenzano is a television personality, author, and creator of the lifestyle online destination FromScratchWithMaria.com. She curates the best in food, craft, family, home decor, and so much more.

FromScratchWithMaria.com is the hub for all of Maria's recipes, crafts, and television appearances. There you can find out about upcoming product launches and get a first look at Maria's latest recipes and projects. Read, shop, get inspired, and subscribe to her weekly newsletter at her website.

My favorite job is soccer mom.

I cry at romantic made-for-TV movies.

If I could eat only one meal for the rest of my life, it would be pasta.

I'm a Michigan girl living in LA, but a farm is where I belong.